Texts Less Traveled

Texts Less Traveled

Exploring Hebrews, the Catholic Epistles, and Revelation

Thomas D. Stegman, SJ

Paulist Press
New York / Mahwah, NJ

Nihil obstat and Imprimatur
Karl J. Kiser, SJ
Provincial, Society of Jesus, U.S. Midwest
July 19, 2021

Cover image by PippW / Shutterstock.com
Cover design by Sharyn Banks
Book design by Lynn Else

Library of Congress Cataloging-in-Publication Data
Names: Stegman, Thomas, author.
Title: Texts less traveled : exploring Hebrews, the Catholic Epistles, and Revelation / Thomas D. Stegman.
Description: New York ; Mahwah, NJ : Paulist Press, [2022] | Summary: "The purpose of this book is to invite and assist readers to embark on a rewarding "journey" through texts in the New Testament that are "less trodden": the Letter to the Hebrews; James; 1 and 2 Peter; 1, 2, and 3 John; Jude; and Revelation"— Provided by publisher.
Identifiers: LCCN 2021048852 (print) | LCCN 2021048853 (ebook) | ISBN 9780809155255 (paperback) | ISBN 9781587689215 (ebook)
Subjects: LCSH: Bible. Hebrews—Commentaries. | Bible. Catholic Epistles—Commentaries. | Bible. Revelation—Commentaries.
Classification: LCC BS2775.53 .S74 2022 (print) | LCC BS2775.53 (ebook) | DDC 227/.8707—dc23/eng/20211117
LC record available at https://lccn.loc.gov/2021048852
LC ebook record available at https://lccn.loc.gov/2021048853

ISBN 978-0-8091-5525-5 (paperback)
ISBN 978-1-58768-921-5 (e-book)

Published by Paulist Press
997 Macarthur Boulevard
Mahwah, New Jersey 07430
www.paulistpress.com

Printed and bound in the
United States of America

I dedicate this book to my surgeon and to all the researchers, doctors, and nurses at Boston Brigham and Women's Hospital and the Dana Farber Cancer Institute who constitute my neuro-oncology healthcare team. Through their unfailing kindnesses and world-class expertise, I have experienced firsthand the compassion and healing work of God. In the course of receiving their care, I have on several occasions mentioned my work on this book. With this dedication, I discharge an oft-expressed promise to render my gratitude to them in writing.

Contents

Acknowledgments ix

Introduction 1

Chapter One—Hebrews 7

Chapter Two—James.. 27

Chapter Three—1 and 2 Peter (Jude) 47

Chapter Four—1, 2, and 3 John... 67

Chapter Five—Revelation 87

Conclusion.. 105

Notes... 111

Acknowledgments

THIS BOOK HAS ITS ORIGINS in a series of articles on the Catholic Epistles I wrote for the *Pastoral Review* in 2011, as well as in a pair of articles on the Letter to the Hebrews I did for the same journal in 2014. The first four chapters in this book are significant expansions of those shorter pieces. I acknowledge with gratitude the kindness of Professor Anthony Towey, the editor of the *Pastoral Review*, for allowing me to use those works as the basis for this book. I also want to thank my friends at Paulist Press for their patience with me, as the writing of this book has been significantly delayed because of major health issues I have experienced since starting it in early summer 2019.

Quotations and citations from Scripture are from the NRSVCE (New Revised Standard Version: Catholic Edition), unless otherwise indicated. Quotations and citations from Vatican II documents are from Austin Flannery (ed.), *Vatican Council II: The Conciliar and Postconciliar Documents*, rev. ed. (Collegeville, MN: Liturgical Press, 1998).

Thomas D. Stegman, SJ
July 16, 2021
Feast of Our Lady of Mount Carmel

Introduction

ONE OF THE MOST FAMOUS—if not *the* most famous—American poems is Robert Frost's "The Road Not Taken."[1] The closing lines, in the poem's fourth and final stanza, are among the best known in American literature:

> Two roads diverged in a wood, and I—
> I took the one less traveled by,
> And that has made all the difference.

In fact, the renown of these lines is such that many people mistakenly call Frost's poem "The Road Less Traveled." Its appeal is that it seemingly calls for taking the risk to try something that the majority passes by, a risk that later is appreciated as rewarding, as making "all the difference."

The purpose of this book is to invite and assist readers to embark on a rewarding "journey" through texts in the New Testament that are less trodden. The texts I have in mind are the Letter to the Hebrews; the Catholic Epistles—James; 1 and 2 Peter; 1, 2, and 3 John; and Jude—so named because, in most cases, the indicated audience is much broader than a particular church community (hence, the audience is more "catholic");[2] and the Book of Revelation. One reason these texts are less traveled is their placement in the New Testament canon.

Texts Less Traveled

A look at the table of contents of the New Testament reveals that it opens with the four Gospels, moves to the story of the early Church as recounted in the Acts of the Apostles, and then transitions to the thirteen writings attributed to St. Paul. The texts less traveled are placed at the *end* of the list, as the final nine (of twenty-seven) writings in the New Testament.

Another reason Hebrews, the Catholic Epistles, and Revelation are less traveled, at least for many Catholics, is that readings from these texts are rarely the subject of preaching in the Church's Sunday eucharistic liturgy. In Ordinary Time, the Gospel reading is coordinated with the first reading, taken from the Old Testament. The second reading—where the texts in question are proclaimed—is on its own cycle and is not coordinated with the Gospel reading. Priests and deacons typically focus their remarks on the Gospel, for understandable reasons. But that means that James (five Sundays in Year B) and Hebrews (seven Sundays in Year B; four more in Year C) are hardly ever commented on. Interestingly, during the Easter Season the Church listens to passages from 1 Peter (Year A), 1 John (Year B), and Revelation (Year C) in the second reading. But truth be told, these texts are seldom the subject of Easter homilies.

A third reason for lighter traffic in Hebrews, the Catholic Epistles, and Revelation is that resources to help guide readers through them are less available, both in terms of quantity and in terms of quality, than those for the Gospels and the Pauline letters. To be sure, the Gospels form the "canon within the canon," the privileged part of the New Testament, for Catholics (evident, for instance, from the proclamation of the word of God at the eucharistic liturgy). One would expect more resources for them. Moreover, the letters attributed to Paul[3] lend themselves to synthetic treatments (e.g., setting forth a Pauline theology), over and beyond the individual letters, which is not the case with the less traveled texts.

The three reasons just outlined are not the only explanation for the lighter traffic in Hebrews, the Catholic Epistles, and Revelation. The texts themselves present a number of puzzles, difficulties, and strange features. For instance, take the Letter to the Hebrews, the subject of chapter 1. The issue of who authored the text has been a source of debate from early on. The great third-century CE biblical scholar Origen ultimately concluded that only "God knows" who wrote it. Among the difficulties in understanding this text is that it operates with a different worldview from ours, Platonism, in which earthly entities are understood to be mere "shadows" of the true heavenly reality. Another challenge is that Hebrews draws heavily on Jewish cultic rituals and sacrifices, including those of the Day of Atonement (Yom Kippur)—something not familiar to most Christians—to present what God has done through Jesus.

Turning to the Letter of James, the focus of chapter 2, the text begins with the identification of the author as "James, a servant of God and of the Lord Jesus Christ." Is this James the figure identified as "the Lord's brother" (Gal 1:19; cf. Mark 6:3), the leader of the early Church in Jerusalem? Or is he some other figure, writing later in the first century CE, as many scholars contend? The text itself appears to be fairly straightforward, offering a series of challenging exhortations on right living. But a peculiar feature of James is that the name "Jesus" is mentioned only twice, including in the opening line quoted above. This fact is one reason why Martin Luther famously described the writing as "an epistle of straw," lacking substance—a notoriously low assessment.

The Petrine letters and Jude, the topics of chapter 3, likewise have some curious characteristics. The elegant style of Greek of 1 Peter has raised the question about how it could have been penned by the apostle, who was an uneducated fisherman from Galilee. While 2 Peter gives the impression of deriving from the same author, evidence internal to the text suggests that it comes from a much later date. For example, the text refers to Paul's letters as a collection and as having the status of Scripture. Second Peter also contains, in its middle section, much of the content of the Letter of Jude, but without some strange references from the latter, such as the archangel Michael contending with the devil over the corpse of Moses. What is the relationship, if any, between 2 Peter and Jude?

Coming to the Johannine letters, the focus of chapter 4, one immediately recognizes a number of motifs and terms from John's Gospel: a prologue in 1 John that highlights the "word of life," God's Son Jesus Christ; God's love revealed in Jesus's humanity; exhortations to walk in the light and truth; and the notions of abiding in God and of God abiding in us. Well and good. But then there is the ominous mention, in 1 and 2 John, of the coming of the "antichrist" and of allusions to schism in the community. The unnamed "elder" who pens 2 John cautions against extending hospitality to false teachers, while he complains in 3 John that he and his emissaries are not being welcomed by someone in an authoritative position in the Johannine community. How to make sense of such division in writings that emphasize the importance of *koinōnia* ("fellowship" or "communion")?

Last, and perhaps most perplexing of all, is the Book of Revelation, the subject of chapter 5. The name of the book derives from the English translation of the first word of the text—*apokalypsis* (from which we get *apocalypse* and *apocalyptic*). Written by a man named John in exile on the island of Patmos, Revelation employs a number of exotic and mystifying figures and features: a slain yet victorious lamb, four horsemen, angels blowing trumpets to unleash plagues, a red dragon, a woman clothed with the sun and crowned with twelve stars, and symbolic numbers (e.g., the infamous 666).

The genre of apocalypse requires much care when offering an interpretation. Indeed, there is a troubling history of interpretation of this text, which includes *mis*interpretations that have led to terrible tragedies. Just think of the massive number of deaths among the Branch Davidians in Waco, Texas, in 1993.

The issue of interpretation brings me back to Frost's poem with which I began this introduction. Notice that I employed the adverb *seemingly* in the last sentence of the opening paragraph. The poem's final lines *seem* to suggest the virtue of setting out on the less traveled road. However, as has recently been argued by literary critics,[4] the poem itself is not so clear-cut. Earlier in the poem, Frost writes that the passing there "had worn them [i.e., the two roads] really about the same." In addition, "both that morning equally lay / In leaves no step had trodden black." So, is one road really less traveled than the other?

It is also crucial to note that the final stanza begins with the poet placing himself in a different point in time, namely, the future—"I shall be telling this with a sigh / Somewhere ages and ages hence." Thus, the determination of taking the road less traveled is an "after the fact" judgment of one looking back in time. Is this the poet's way of saying that people try to make sense of their lives in retrospect, explaining things in order to give their lives coherence and meaning? If this is the case, then is the typical reading that I set forth at the outset wrong? Or does the ambiguity allow for multiple readings?

Now, my purpose here is not to offer an authoritative interpretation of "The Road Not Taken" (which is beyond my competence) but to illustrate the importance of a close, thoughtful reading of texts. If this is true of a poem about a walk in the woods, how much more is it the case when it comes to reading texts that we regard as the word of God, including Hebrews, the Catholic Epistles, and Revelation—with all the challenges and difficulties mentioned above? My hope is that the following chapters will encourage and assist readers to engage in a careful, prayerful reading of these less traveled texts. These texts are worth such a reading because they contain a number of inspiring images and teachings that can deeply nourish the life of faith. We ought not to be deterred by the challenges and difficulties.

The format of this book is similar to the one I have used in two previous works: *Opening the Door of Faith*, which is largely about the Gospels and Acts of the Apostles; and *Written for Our Instruction*, which is about St. Paul's teaching, mostly via the Letter to the Romans. Each chapter begins with a brief overview of the writing(s) in question, and then I propose four key themes found in them that I proceed to develop. These themes focus chiefly on the portrayal of Jesus and on Christian living in light of what God has done through his Son and the gift of the Spirit. At the end of each chapter are discussion questions to facilitate further reflection—preferably done with others.

I want to be clear that this book is not intended to substitute for reading the biblical texts themselves, but rather to provide assistance for appreciating the life of faith proposed in them. You may consider reading first the biblical text in question before reading my analysis. Or, if you prefer, you can use my presentation as an entry point for your study. The internal biblical citations are intended as an aid, though some readers might find it easier to pass over them.

In the concluding chapter, I gather and summarize the major points. In particular, I highlight all the things we would miss out on if we did not traverse these less traveled texts. The benefits and gains are considerable. I am confident that, when we arrive at the end of the journey, we will find that it makes, if not *all* the difference, at least a significant difference in our understanding of the life of faith and the way of discipleship.

CHAPTER ONE

Hebrews

BEFORE THE THREE-YEAR lectionary cycle appeared in 1969 (as mandated by Vatican II), the liturgical proclamation of passages from Hebrews was introduced by the formula "A reading from the Letter of St. Paul to the Hebrews." This formulation was inaccurate on three counts. First, the writing is not from St. Paul, but from an anonymous figure, one who (like Paul) was well versed in the Old Testament and skilled in rhetorical argument.[1] Second, while the text concludes with epistolary conventions, the author himself more accurately describes his work as a "word of exhortation" (13:22). In other words, the text is a homily that interweaves biblical and theological exposition with pastoral applications. Third, the audience is not "Hebrews" but, rather, a community of Jews who had become Christ-believers.

More specifically, the author writes to a group of Jewish Christians who had previously endured persecution and suffering. Some had been imprisoned; others had property confiscated (10:32–34). Moreover, it appears that such opposition was still a possibility in the present. As a result of suffering for their faith, some members were becoming discouraged. One manifestation of their discouragement was to stop coming to the community's liturgical gathering (10:25). Whether they were inclined to return to Jewish worship and practice is not clear. Also not clear are the location of the community in question and the date of composition. A reference to Italy in 13:24 suggests to some that the community in question was in Rome. Most scholars date the writing toward the end of the first century, between 70 and 90 CE.

The author of Hebrews responds to the situation by reminding the community what God has done in and through Jesus. He then attempts to persuade them to respond appropriately. In what follows, I focus first on the author's portrayal of Jesus as God's eternal Son, as the pioneer and perfecter of faith, and as the fulfillment of Scripture. This leads to one of the unique features of Hebrews: the presentation of Jesus as high priest and his sacrificial offering via imagery from the Day of Atonement. Then will follow implications for the community: their identity as God's new covenant people, a sojourning people who walk by faithful hope; and the call to maturation and "training" in the way of discipleship.

JESUS: GOD'S SON, "PIONEER AND PERFECTER" OF FAITH, AND FULFILLMENT OF SCRIPTURE

The opening lines of Hebrews offer a number of exalted descriptions of God's Son. Of great significance is the author's depiction of God's having *spoken* through his Son (1:2). Jesus is the revelation of God, the most profound manifestation of who God is and how God reaches out to human beings. The metaphor of God's speaking through his Son Jesus conveys something very important about God: God is self-revelatory in a personal and relational way. This personal and relational manner is grounded in love, for love by its very nature seeks to self-reveal. It is this personal-relational modality of God's self-revelation in love that was adopted by the fathers at Vatican II, especially in *Dei Verbum*, the Dogmatic Constitution on Divine Revelation.

Hebrews makes clear that God is the creator who made all things by his word (11:3; cf. Gen 1:1—2:3). God's word is powerful and life-giving. The author famously describes this word as "living and active [*energēs*, from which we derive the word *energy*], sharper than any two-edged sword" (4:12). God's word is so formidable that it can even raise the dead to life (11:19). Strikingly, Hebrews presents the Son as the one through whom God created the world (1:2), an allusion to the Son's preexistence. Moreover, the Son's powerful word *sustains* creation (1:3). The Son's participation in the work of creation places him above all things, including the angels. The text thus makes abundantly clear the intimate relationship between Father and Son, the latter of whom is "the reflection of God's glory and the exact imprint of God's very being" (1:3).

More subtly, Hebrews reveals God as one who enters into covenant relationship. The author refers to the promises made to Abraham (6:13–14) and to the covenant made with Israel at Sinai through Moses (3:3–5; 9:18–22). As we will see shortly, he also cites the celebrated passage in Jeremiah about God's establishing a "new covenant" with his people (8:8–12; Jer 13:31–34), now through Jesus, "the mediator of a new covenant" (Heb 9:15; 12:24). While it is true that Hebrews insists on the superiority of the new covenant to the Sinai covenant, it is also imperative to appreciate "the unchangeable character of [God's] purpose" (6:17) as shown forth in the divine impetus toward covenant. The essential point is that God, as definitively revealed by Jesus, is characterized by his desire to be in relationship with people and to form them in holiness (12:14; Lev 19:2).

What makes Jesus's mediation of the new covenant possible is his becoming human. One of the more intriguing appellations of Jesus is found in Hebrews 3:1, where the author describes him as "apostle." As *apostolos*, Jesus has been *sent* (the meaning of the Greek term) by God. More specifically, he was sent as one in full solidarity with the children of "flesh and blood" (2:14). Hebrews thereby gives no rein to any docetic interpretation of Jesus, one that would denigrate his humanity. Jesus entered completely into the human condition, becoming "like his brothers and sisters in every respect" (2:17). He thereby confirms the inherent goodness and dignity of human beings, who are created in God's image and likeness (Gen 1:27).

Like all human beings, Jesus suffered and was tempted. There is one respect, however, in which he is not like other people: Jesus did not sin (Heb 4:15; 7:26; 9:14). Yet his sinlessness should not be interpreted as his being above the fray of human struggle. The text declares that "in the days of his flesh, Jesus offered up prayers and supplications, with loud cries and tears, to the one who was able to save him from death, and he was heard because of his reverent submission" (5:7). This statement alludes to his prayer in Gethsemane. It also suggests his manner of prayer throughout his life. Such prayer is indicative of Jesus's fundamental posture of obedience to God his Father: "Then I said, 'See, God, I have come to do your will, O God'" (10:7, citing Ps 40:8).

This obedience was hard earned, coming at a great price. The author of Hebrews states that Jesus "*learned* obedience through what he suffered" (Heb 5:8) and that he was "made perfect" (5:9; cf. 2:10). The phrase "made perfect" translates the Greek word *teleiōtheis* that indicates a *process*, one that was aided by God, as indicated by the use of the divine passive.[2] Therefore it is no surprise that the author later describes Jesus as the "pioneer and perfecter [*teleiōthēs*] of our faith" (12:2; cf. 2:10). As the "pioneer" of our faith, Jesus has led the way by blazing the trail and path of obedience to God, even in the face of suffering and death. As the "perfecter" of our faith, his death is the fullest expression of obedience that has now created the possibility of our walking in such faithfulness, a point to which we will return later in the chapter.

Although God spoke "long ago" through the prophets (1:1), Hebrews insists that the prophetic word of Scripture *continues* to speak in the present. The author interprets a number of Old Testament texts through the lens of what God has done through Jesus. For example, he reads texts originally composed for the coronation of Israel's kings as messianic passages referring to Jesus. That is, he cites Psalm 2:7 to highlight Jesus's unique, intimate relationship with God: "You are my Son; / today I have begotten you" (Heb 1:5; 5:5). He employs Psalm 110:1 in reference to the heavenly exaltation of Jesus: "Sit at my right hand / until I make your enemies a footstool for your feet" (Heb 1:13; 10:13). Similarly, he reads Psalm 45:7, a royal wedding psalm, as signaling Jesus's anointing as the Messiah (= Christ, "the anointed one"): "You have loved righteousness and hated wickedness; / therefore God, your God, has anointed you / with the oil of gladness beyond your companions" (Heb 1:9).

A classic illustration of the way the author of Hebrews reads texts christologically is his treatment in 2:5–9 of Psalm 8. This psalm proclaims the beauty and grandeur of God's creation and expresses wonderment at the privileged role given to human beings to exercise stewardship over it (e.g., "What are human beings that you are mindful of them?"). Hebrews, however, interprets the notice of the "son of man"[3] being made lower than angels for a little while as a reference to Jesus's incarnation, to his becoming human in order to "taste death for everyone" (Heb 2:9). The psalm also mentions the crowning of this figure with glory and the subjection of all things to him, which the author reads as indicating Jesus's heavenly exaltation.

The ancient biblical texts not only prophesy what God has already done through Jesus; they also specify what is yet to come. Hebrews combines Isaiah 26:20 and Habakkuk 2:3 to indicate the return in glory of the risen Jesus: "For yet 'in a very little while, / the one who is coming will come and will not delay'" (Heb 10:37; cf. 9:28). Thus, for the author, there are Old Testament texts that point to the second coming of Jesus.

In addition to citing various passages, the author refers to a number of persons and figures from Scripture to shed light on Jesus and his significance. One example is in 3:5–6, where he discusses Moses's role as the faithful "servant" of the "house"—that is, of the people, Israel—that God "built." Moses is also described there as the one chosen "to testify to the things that would be spoken later." The latter's prophetic role is thereby highlighted, pointing to Messiah Jesus, who is now "faithful over God's house as a son." That is, through Jesus's faithfulness as God's obedient Son, God has formed the new covenant people. The effect of all this is to show that the sacred texts find their full realization in Jesus the Messiah and that he provides the interpretative key to Scripture.

JESUS THE HIGH PRIEST AND SACRIFICE

The dynamics of the author's christological reading of Scripture coalesce in his portrait of Jesus as the eternal high priest. Hebrews lists three essential qualities of a high priest (5:1–4): he is chosen from the people; he must be able to sympathize with human weakness; and he is called by God for the office. The high priest was appointed to offer gifts and sacrifices (8:3). The sacrifice par excellence to be offered was the one on the Day of Atonement (Yom Kippur). On that day, the high priest entered the inner sanctuary of the temple, the "Holy of Holies"—wherein were the ark of the covenant with the tablets on which were written the Ten Commandments and the mercy seat that was overshadowed by the cherubim of glory. The high priest took with him sacrificial blood (from animals) that he offered and sprinkled for sins, including his own (9:1–10; cf. Lev 16:1–34).

All this is background for the presentation of Jesus as high priest. For the author of Hebrews, what I have just described is but "a sketch and shadow" (Heb 8:5) of the true Holy Place, the heavenly sanctuary "not made with hands" (9:11). Here we get a flavor of the author's Platonic worldview, in which earthly, material things are less "real" than the heavenly and spiritual realm.[4] Hebrews insists that Messiah Jesus "entered into heaven itself, now to appear in the presence of God on our behalf" (9:24). As the true high priest, Jesus "entered once for all...with his own blood, thus obtaining eternal redemption" (9:12). It is "the sacrifice of himself" (9:26), the one "without blemish" (i.e., without sin; 9:14), that has effected the removal and forgiveness of sins—something the prior sacrifices could not do.

The portrayal of Jesus as high priest is not without problems, however, as the author knows only too well. Why? Because Jesus was descended from Judah, a tribe "from which no one has ever served at the altar" (7:13–14). He was not from the priestly tribe of Levi. Here the author offers a daring, ingenious solution. He appeals to the mysterious figure of Melchizedek (7:1–28), who makes a brief appearance in the story of Abraham (Gen 14:18–20). This priestly figure brought out bread and wine when he came to bless Abraham, after which the latter gave him tithes, one-tenth of all he had. Melchizedek is also referred to in Psalm 110:4—"You are a priest forever according to the order of Melchizedek"—a text the author interprets as referring to Jesus (Heb 5:6; 7:17).

As "king of righteousness" (the meaning of the name "Melchizedek") and "king of peace" (derived from the name "Salem"), Melchizedek foreshadows Jesus as the one who enacts God's will—that is what it means to be "righteous"—

and who brings about true and lasting *shalom* with God and with others. The fact that Melchizedek blessed Abraham and received tithes from him shows his superiority to Abraham and, by extension, to the latter's descendant Levi (Heb 7:4–10). Most telling is that Melchizedek is "without genealogy, having neither beginning of days nor end of life" (7:3). For the author, it is "the power of an indestructible life" that is the true warrant for authentic priesthood, not blood descent (7:15–17). He thereby sets forth, via Melchizedek, an order of priesthood prior to and greater than the Levitical priesthood.

It is significant to observe that Hebrews links Jesus's sacrificial offering with the notion of "new covenant." The New Testament's longest quotation of a passage from the Jewish Scriptures is found in 8:8–12, where the author cites Jeremiah 31:31–34. This famous passage relates God's promise to establish a new covenant with his people, one marked by the transformation of human hearts and the forgiveness of sins: "For I will be merciful toward their iniquities, / and I will remember their sins no more" (Heb 8:12; cf. Jer 31:34). This promise of transformation and of the forgiveness of sins has now been realized through the ministrations of Jesus the high priest. Whereas the Sinai covenant was inaugurated by Moses sprinkling the blood of goats and calves (Heb 9:18–22), the new covenant has been initiated by the sanctifying "sprinkled blood" of Jesus, "the mediator of a new covenant" (12:24).

Jesus's priesthood is unique in that he is also the sacrifice. His blood, shed "once for all" (7:27; 9:26; 10:10), is the acceptable sacrifice. In addition to bringing about "atonement for the sins of the people" (2:17) and sanctification (i.e., our being made holy through the gift of the Holy Spirit; 10:10 and 13:12), Jesus's sacrifice has effected a freedom that the author describes in a striking manner in 2:15. There he declares that Jesus died in order to "free those who all their lives were held in slavery by the fear of death." This statement calls for reflection. It suggests that it is our fear of death that leads us to grasp after "life" where it is not offered—whether that be riches, reputation, power over others, the fulfillment of pleasures, etcetera. Pursuit of these things, as if they are what truly give happiness and life, ultimately leads to our becoming enslaved in sinful habits. The "once for all" sacrifice of Jesus has freed us from the root cause, the fear of death. And it leads us to receive life from the only true source, God.

Jesus's sacrificial death, of course, is not the end of the story, nor is it the full expression of his high priestly ministry. God "brought back from the dead our Lord Jesus" (13:20), thereby vindicating his faithful obedience and endurance of suffering "for the sake of the joy that was set before him" (12:2). Jesus is thus the "forerunner" of those who hope in the fullness of life (6:19–20). Exalted in heavenly glory and seated at God's right hand (7:26; 10:12), Jesus now reigns over "the house [i.e., the people] of God" (10:21).

More specifically, Jesus reigns as the exalted high priest. The author of Hebrews suggests two aspects of Jesus's heavenly priesthood. The first aspect, which culminates the portrayal of his sacrificial death, is—as mentioned earlier—the risen Jesus's entrance into "the greater and more perfect" sanctuary, the heavenly "Holy Place," with the offering of his own blood (9:11–14). This "once for all" offering of life and blood has brought about the reconciliation between God and humankind, as well as the purification from sins, that the celebration of the Day of Atonement foreshadowed.

This unsurpassable sacrifice, however, does not exhaust the exercise of Jesus's priestly ministry. In addition to offering gifts and sacrifices for sins, the role of a priest is to advocate to God for the benefit of people. Indeed, the second aspect of Jesus's priestly ministry is his intercession to God on our behalf: "he is able for all time to save those who approach God through him, since he always lives to make intercession for them" (7:25). Whereas Matthew's Gospel presents Jesus as Emmanuel, "God-with-us" (see Matt 1:23; cf. Isa 7:14), the author of Hebrews depicts the Son as God-*for*-us.

Because Jesus entered fully into the human condition, and because he has suffered and known what it is like to be tempted, as high priest he is able to be compassionate and sympathize with human weakness (Heb 4:15). Moreover, he readily renders help and support to those who are being tested (2:18). The author therefore encourages his readers to approach with confidence and boldness "the throne of grace" in order to "receive mercy and find grace to help in time of need" (4:16). This is, to say the least, a beautiful and inspiring portrait of Jesus that offers hope and consolation. Jesus the eternal, merciful high priest *continues* to mediate God's covenant love and bestowal of life. For this reason, it can be said that he is "the same yesterday and today and forever" (13:8).

THE SOJOURNING NEW COVENANT PEOPLE WHO WALK IN FAITHFUL HOPE

While Hebrews provides the basis for a rich understanding of Jesus, the text is not a christological treatise per se. As the author states at the end of the work, he has written a "word of exhortation" (13:22). That is, he attempts to encourage his audience to *respond* appropriately to God in light of what God has done through Jesus. In fact, Hebrews is saturated with inferential particles (especially the small Greek words *oun* and *dio*) that are best rendered "therefore" (2:1; 3:1, 7; 4:1, 11, 14, 16; 6:1; 10:19, 35; 12:1, 12, 28; 13:13). For example—and as we have just seen—after describing Jesus as the high priest who, having known temptation, is able to sympathize with our weakness, the author urges, "Let us *therefore* approach the throne of grace with boldness" (4:16).

The frequent employment of inferential particles is a significant part of the rhetorical strategy of Hebrews. The author's goal is to persuade his readers to mature in their reception and appropriation of God's decisive revelation through the death and resurrection of Jesus (6:1). In other words, he is concerned with growing in the life of discipleship. And the life of discipleship is one that is, in the first place, a communal reality. In fact, we are indebted to this writing for its important contribution to ecclesiology, to the topic of what is the Church.

We noted above that God's covenantal love is a theme that subtly pervades the text, as seen by the allusions to the Sinai covenant through which God entered into a special relationship with the people Israel. In spite of the people's infidelities, God's covenant faithfulness endures, as indicated by Jeremiah's prophecy about the "new covenant" with the house of Israel. This prophecy has been fulfilled through Jesus's atoning death and resurrection, as well as through the outpouring of the Holy Spirit. Those who open their hearts to "so great a salvation" (2:3) have their sins forgiven and their consciences purified (10:22) and are made partakers of the Spirit. In short, they are constituted as members of God's (new) covenant people. This is their identity.

That the identity of covenant people is important in Hebrews is evident from the number of references to holiness. God's people are to be distinguished by holiness (cf. Lev 19:2—"You shall be holy, for I the LORD your God am holy"). The author of Hebrews constantly reminds his readers that they have been "sanctified" (literally, "made holy") by the blood of Christ (Heb 2:11; 10:10, 14; 13:12). Because they have been made sharers in the Holy Spirit (6:4), the author—like St. Paul—refers to them as *hagioi*, "holy ones" (au. trans. of 3:1; 6:10).[5] And since they are blessed in these ways, they are called to grow in holiness (12:14). Holiness, of course, is

17

one of the four "marks" of the Church set forth in the Nicene Creed ("one, *holy*, catholic, and apostolic").

Another crucial identity marker of God's people is that they are "sojourners" (au. trans. of 11:13) who seek a heavenly "homeland" (*patris*, from which we get "fatherland"; 11:14; cf. 13:14 and "the city that is to come"). That is, they are a pilgrim people who in this life and world are "on the way." Vatican II picked up on this image of pilgrim people. *Lumen Gentium*, the Dogmatic Constitution on the Church, devotes an entire chapter to "The Pilgrim Church" (nos. 48–51). This image of a sojourning pilgrim people lies in the background of the author's exhortation, "Let us *therefore* make every effort to enter that rest," that is, the heavenly homeland (4:11).

The language of "entering into God's rest" is taken from Psalm 95 (v. 11), a psalm from which the author of Hebrews cites at length in 3:7–11. The beginning of that citation is "*Today*, if you hear his [i.e., God's] voice, / do not harden your hearts" (see Ps 95:7). Significantly, the author focuses on the force of "today," insisting that this text, along with all of Scripture, can speak afresh to us each day—granted that we are listening carefully. Recall that God's word is "living and active" (Heb 4:12). The story of Scripture, while fulfilled in Jesus, is to *continue* in the lives of the pilgrim people, the Church. The words of Psalm 118:5 quoted in 13:6—"The Lord is my helper; / I will not be afraid. / What can anyone to do me?"—apply to us today as much as they did in their original context. So too do the words of the Habakkuk 2:4 set forth in 10:38—"my righteous one will live by faith."

Habakkuk's reference to "faith" or "faithfulness" (*pistis*) leads the author to make one of his most important contributions. In Hebrews 11:1 he sets forth his famous definition of *faith*: "Faith is the assurance of things hoped for, the conviction of things not seen." Notice the role hope plays in this definition. To be sure, hope is a prominent theme in Hebrews (see, e.g., 3:6; 6:11; 7:19). The basis for hope is the resurrection and exaltation of Jesus, who has gone as a forerunner into the heavenly sanctuary. This basis grounds the author's exhortation to "seize the hope set before us" (6:18). The life of faith moves toward the horizon of resurrection hope. Hope in the resurrection is necessary because the way of faithfulness, as set forth in this text, is not easy. Moreover, such hope enables buoyancy and sustains endurance when our commitment to follow Jesus leads to opposition, misunderstanding, and suffering.

The entire eleventh chapter (vv. 1–40) of Hebrews is an encomium in praise of faith. It presents a veritable "hall of fame" of biblical figures who modeled heroic faith. Chief among these are Abraham and Moses. Abraham is the archetypal sojourner who left all behind to follow God's call wherever it led him, all the while "living in tents" (11:8–10). He and his wife Sarah trusted in God, old age and all other evidence to the contrary, to fulfill God's promise of a son (11:11–12). Even more, Abraham was later willing to offer up to God this son, Isaac, the heir through whom his promised descendants were to come. He trusted God and "considered the fact that God is able even to raise someone from the dead—and figuratively speaking, he did receive him back" (11:17–19).

The author describes incidents from Moses's life that make him a prototype of Jesus. Rather than opt for a life of privilege, luxury, and pleasure in the family of Pharaoh, Moses chose to be in solidarity with God's people, sharing in their ill treatment (11:24–25). Strikingly, Moses is depicted as suffering for the sake of the Messiah: "He considered abuse suffered for the Christ to be greater wealth than the treasures of Egypt, for he was looking ahead to the reward" (11:26). Anticipating the way of Jesus, he did not cower before the powerful (in his case, the king of Egypt) but rather obeyed God's commands in delivering the people from oppression in a surprising fashion, against all odds (11:27–29).

The impressive catalog of "so great a cloud of witnesses" who lived in faithful hope in the face of challenges and suffering culminates with an exhortation that alters the metaphor of sojourning to that of running a race: "*Therefore...* let us run with perseverance the race that is set before us" (12:1). Here is the place where the author of Hebrews names Jesus as "the pioneer and perfecter of our faith" (12:2), the one who endured the cross and its shame because he trusted in God to vindicate his fidelity. Jesus focused on "the joy that was set before him"—enthronement at God's right hand—all appearances to the contrary (12:2). His self-offering on the cross was the climax of his commitment to do God's will (10:5–7). God's sojourning, new covenant people are to follow the lead of Jesus (12:2). The life of discipleship is ultimately *imitatio Christi*.

MATURATION IN DISCIPLESHIP BY "TRAINING" AND "EXERCISE"

What does running the race with perseverance look like concretely? First, it is important to indicate what it does *not* mean. The image of being a pilgrim people in a world in which "we have no lasting city" (13:14) might give the impression that God's people are not to participate or be involved in the nitty-gritty of life. That would be a false impression. *Gaudium et Spes*, the Pastoral Constitution on the Church, insists that in our sojourn to the heavenly city, we should be moved to "a greater commitment to working with all people towards the establishment of a world that is more human" (*GS* 57). The Church does so as "the universal sacrament of salvation" that witnesses to and actualizes God's love for all (*LG* 48; *GS* 45).

Returning to Hebrews, recall the context that occasioned the writing. The author refers to sufferings endured in the past, such as imprisonment and loss of property (10:32–34), by some members of the community on account of their faith commitment. Reading between the lines, it seems that such sufferings were also a present possibility, which would explain, at least in part, the sense of discouragement some were feeling. Opposition against and persecution of Christians certainly happen in parts of the world today. Even where they do not, the specific exhortations in the final chapter (13:1–6) are apropos.

The author begins with a general call to brotherly/sisterly love (*philadelphia*). He then fills out this call by encouraging his readers "to show hospitality to strangers" and to "remember those who are in prison" (13:1–3). This calls for greater awareness of and sensitivity to those who are suffering, and for commitment to reach out to them in solidarity. The appeal to hospitality to strangers has particular relevance in the present context of debates on immigration and refugee policies. We would do well to recall the author's suggestion that in welcoming such people, "some have entertained angels without knowing it" (13:1; cf. Gen 18:1–15). Ministry to the imprisoned—not to mention, to the sick, shut-ins, and others who are marginalized—is, as the Gospel writer Matthew reveals, ministry to Jesus himself (Matt 25:31–46).

The next exhortation is a call to faithfulness in marriage, a call that easily extends to fidelity in *all* relationships (Heb 13:4). The author then warns against the "love of money," that is, against the idols of possessions and false security. Instead, community members are to be content with what they have. This is an appeal to simplicity of life, to a way and standard of living that do not come at the expense or exploitation of others. It is also an implicit appeal to generosity. The author grounds it with a line from Joshua 1:5 that conveys God's promise, "I will never leave you or forsake you" (Heb 13:5). This quotation reminds us of God's providential love and care, which can be at work through our generosity and concern for the marginalized. Such self-giving love aligns with the sacrifice of Jesus. This is what holiness looks like.

The way of faith presented in Hebrews is arduous, to say the least. A particular challenge is the author's constant emphasis on suffering. Suffering has different dimensions. The previous two paragraphs have proposed ways in which we can sacrifice for the sake of others (in part, to alleviate their suffering). To place another's agenda and needs as on a par with mine—or even as more urgent—is a form of sacrifice. It can come at personal cost. It is also something I actively *choose* to do. To suffer opposition because of faith convictions is a different type of suffering, as it comes from without; it is something *endured*. People who have been taunted and ridiculed, and even arrested, for taking a courageous stand—such as for the right to life, for racial and social justice, for disarmament and peace—know this kind of suffering. Jesus's offering his life on the cross encapsulated both chosen and endured aspects. He gave himself in love and suffered "hostility against himself" (12:3).

Recall the presentation of Jesus as one who *learned* obedience through suffering and who was made perfect (5:8–9). Implicit in this portrayal is the theme of God who, as Father, "disciplines" or "trains" (*paideuei*) those whom he loves (12:5–6; cf. Prov 3:11)—including his Son. This notion of parental discipline is, to say the least, controversial in many circles today. In order to give a sympathetic reading to the author's portrayal and to derive benefit from it, we need to appreciate what underlies *paideia*. The term denotes the laborious process of training and educating children (*pais*, "child," is the root of the word). Optimally, *paideia* issues forth from fierce parental love, a love that seeks what is truly best for one's child. It is no accident that the Greek word for "disciple" is *mathētēs*, which means "learner" or "pupil."

Immediately following his reference to Jesus as the "pioneer and perfecter [*teleiōthēs*] of our faith," the author turns to the theme of *paideia* in 12:3–11 for the life of discipleship. In fact, this passage is replete with *paid*-terminology (eight instances). In order to inculcate "maturity" (au. trans. of the word *teleiotēs* in 6:1) among his readers, he focuses on the importance of training and discipline. He interprets their suffering through the lens of *paideia*. In 12:7 he exhorts them to endure trials for the sake of discipline, saying, "God is treating you as children." This statement requires much care because it can be misused and abused (e.g., it can lead to a false understanding of God as one who capriciously causes people to suffer).[6]

I propose that we think about divine training through the concept of "spiritual exercises." The word translated "trained" in 12:11 is *gymnazō*, from which we get our words *gymnastics* and *gymnasium*. It evokes physical exercise that, while difficult and painful at times, results in good condition and health. Engagement in *spiritual* exercises—praying, growing in virtuous habits, practicing acts of mercy—likewise requires commitment, discipline, and sacrifice. Over time, such exercises will result in our ability to enact with greater ease and joy the ways of self-giving love discussed above, "the peaceful fruit of righteousness" (12:11). Spiritual exercises can also strengthen us to persevere when our faith commitment leads us into conflict and opposition from without. When we allow ourselves to be so "trained," with God's help, we mature in our identity and status as his children. It is demanding, but we are invited to draw near to the throne of grace to "receive mercy and find grace to help" (4:16) from our high priest and advocate, Jesus.

This reference to mercy and grace leads to a final word about Hebrews. At several points, the author warns of the dire consequences of turning away from God after having received the good news of salvation (2:1–3; 6:4–8; 10:26–31; 12:25–27). The issue is expressed most baldly as follows: "For it is impossible to restore again to repentance those who...have shared in the Holy Spirit...and then have fallen away" (6:4–6). Does God's mercy have limits? The author's description of the atonement of sins through Jesus's death speaks eloquently of its efficaciousness. There is no sin God cannot or will not forgive, granted that one turns to God for mercy—and, if need be, *returns* to do so. If there is any shortcoming in mercy, it is on the human side if we close and harden our hearts to God. The new covenant inaugurated through Jesus is characterized by God's mercy and forgiveness (8:12). God's pilgrim people constantly drink from the wellsprings of this mercy as they sojourn and train in the ways of holiness.

QUESTIONS FOR PRAYER AND REFLECTION

1. Why is it important to appreciate that God's impetus toward self-revelation is rooted in love? How have I experienced God's personal-relational manner of self-revelation?

2. When I think about Jesus in his humanity, what immediately comes to mind? How does the presentation of Jesus as the pioneer and perfecter of our faith make me appreciate more his humanity? What do I make of Jesus's *learning* obedience?

3. How does the portrayal of Jesus as both high priest and sacrifice speak to me? Why is it important to understand the background of the Day of Atonement in this portrayal?

4. How can the image of Jesus as compassionate intercessor help me to trust more in God's mercy and forgiveness? What can help me to approach Jesus with greater confidence?

5. In what ways does the author's understanding of the fear of death (2:15) resonate with me? How can I allow Jesus to free me from that fear?

6. What comes to mind when I think of the word *holiness*? How does Hebrews inspire me to grow in holiness?

7. How does the concept "pilgrim people" speak to me? What is there in this image that helps me? Inspires me? Causes me discomfort?

8. Why is hope so important for the life of faith? Who and what have given me hope? For what do I most hope?

9. How does Hebrews help me to appreciate God's word as living and active? In what ways can I see the story of Scripture continuing in me and in my faith community?

10. How can the notions of divine training and spiritual exercises inform my discipleship? My understanding of the role of suffering in Christian life?

CHAPTER TWO

James

THE FIRST OF THE CATHOLIC Epistles in the New Testament canon is the Letter of James. Unlike Hebrews, whose author is anonymous, the writer of this text is named at the outset: "James, a servant of God and of the Lord Jesus Christ" (1:1). The "James" in question is probably not either of the two apostles of Jesus with that name (James, son of Zebedee; or James, son of Alphaeus). Rather, he is the James to whom Paul refers as "the Lord's brother" (Gal 1:19).[1] Like Paul, he was the recipient of a revelation of the risen Lord (1 Cor 15:7). This James became the most prominent leader of the early Church in Jerusalem (cf. Acts 15:13–21; Gal 2:9, 12). Does this writing derive from the life and ministry of James, or does it come from someone writing later in his name? The manner in which the author employs Jesus-traditions (see below) and the intense expectation of the return of the Lord (Jas 5:8) indicate, at least to me, that the former is more probable. If so, the text was likely penned in the 50s CE (James was martyred ca. 62 CE).

The author identifies himself as a teacher (3:1). James is a teacher of wisdom who imparts advice on how to live a good life. While the text begins with an epistolary greeting, it is best described as wisdom instruction. The opening chapter introduces the topics to be covered—God's generous provision, the importance of prayer, the danger of riches, the proper use of the tongue, putting conviction into practice, and care for the most vulnerable. The remainder of the text is a series of essays or mini-lectures that develop these topics. James emphasizes the need for "endurance," since the goal in life is to mature in the way of wisdom (1:2–4). The audience—named as "the twelve tribes in the Dispersion" (1:1)—was likely Jewish Christian in makeup (cf. the term *synagōgē*, "synagogue" [NRSV, "assembly"] in 2:2). "Dispersion" is used in a spiritual sense, indicating being away from our heavenly homeland.

As we will see, James sets forth a robust theology—an understanding of who God is and how God acts—that undergirds everything in the text. Although the writing contains only two instances of the name Jesus, Christology plays an important role in the exposition; so too does the author's insistence on the need for works to animate the life of faith. Next, I treat two key interrelated themes, friendship with God and the wisdom from above, which will lead to a look at James's exhortations that both challenge and comfort. While the text is largely an instruction in wisdom, we will also discover in it a strong prophetic voice that can be unsettling.

JAMES'S *THEOLOGY* AS FOUNDATIONAL TO HIS TEACHING

The topic of God (*theos*, from which we get *theology*) lies at the heart of James's teaching. The first divine quality the author names is God's lavish generosity. When it comes to bestowing wisdom, James says that God is willing to give "to all generously and ungrudgingly" (1:5). Observe how this description points to two aspects of God's largesse. First, God desires to be munificent to *all*; no one is excluded from God's purview. Second, God gives *gladly*; his generosity is unstinting. Implicit here is divine love. Love by its nature does not coerce or force itself on others. Love offers itself freely, and James states (by means of the example of wisdom) that it is bestowed on those who are open to it (1:6). To be sure, God's beneficence goes beyond the bestowal of wisdom: "*Every* generous act of giving, with every perfect gift, is from above, coming down from the Father of lights" (1:17). Notice that God is called "Father" (1:27; 3:9), a description that evokes a loving parent who wants the best for his or her children.

The portrayal of God as "Father of lights" suggests his role as Creator. God is the creator of the sun, the moon, and the stars that mark the times and seasons (Gen 1:14–18) and manifest his grandeur (cf., e.g., Ps 19:6). Light is also evocative of the divine presence and glory: "The LORD is my light and my salvation" (Ps 27:1). Indeed, in chapter 5 we will see that God's presence in the "new Jerusalem" will be such that "there will be no more night; they need no light of lamp or sun, for the Lord God will be their light" (Rev 22:5). James calls God "the Father of lights, with whom there is no variation or shadow due to change" (Jas 1:17). What this depiction emphasizes is God's transcendence and superiority over creation. There is only one God (2:19) who is judge of all (4:12).

James goes on, in 1:18, to use a maternal metaphor to describe God's creation of human beings: God "gave us birth by the word of truth." This female image evokes a mother's love for her child. What does the phrase "by the word of truth," the *means* by which God has created, indicate? At one level, "the word" points to God's creation of human beings by the power of his word (Gen 1:26–29). At another level, "the word of *truth*" refers to God's creation of a special people through the gift of the law revealed to Moses, a point to which I will return momentarily. Moreover, as will become more evident in the next section, "the word of *truth*" also signifies the message of the gospel—the good news about what God has done in and through Jesus—that has brought the Church into being.

"The word of truth" in the second sense above suggests the notion of law and the role of God as lawgiver (see Jas 4:12). And this, in turn, evokes the concept of *covenant*. God is a covenant God who seeks to be in relationship with a people who are called to manifest his holiness to others, as succinctly set forth in Leviticus 19:2—"You shall be holy, for I the LORD your God am holy." In fact, James cites a commandment from the same chapter of Leviticus in 2:8: "You shall love your neighbor as yourself" (Lev 19:18). All of Leviticus 19 presents ways God's people are to grow in holiness. Strikingly, a number of prohibitions found in that chapter are taken up by James (e.g., prohibitions against false oaths, defrauding others of wages, showing partiality, and slandering others). The point to appreciate is that God is covenantal. That is, God is a relational God who teaches and leads his people to holiness. He is no "unmoved mover," as the phrase "with whom there is no variation" might suggest.

That God is not an unmoved mover is also evident from James's description in 5:11 of God as "compassionate and merciful." The quoted words evoke God's famous self-revelation to Moses in Exodus 34:6: "The LORD, the LORD, / a God merciful and gracious, / slow to anger, / and abounding in steadfast love and faithfulness." In 5:4 James warns that "the cries of the [defrauded] harvesters have reached the ears of the Lord of hosts" (cf. Exod 3:7). God has a special love and concern for the poor, whom he has chosen "to be rich in faith and to be heirs of the kingdom that he has promised to those who love him" (Jas 2:5). In fact, James suggests that there will come a time when God acts definitively in judgment to raise up the lowly and to bring down the rich (1:9; cf. Mary's *Magnificat* in Luke 1:46–55). The author cites with approval the Greek version of

Proverbs 3:34—"God opposes the proud, / but gives grace to the humble" (Jas 4:6).

This last citation leads to an exegetical point I learned from my teacher and dissertation director, Luke Timothy Johnson.[2] The NRSV is typical in translating the previous verse, 4:5, as saying, "God yearns jealously for the spirit that he has made to dwell in us." It is true that the word *zēlos* can have both positive (i.e., be zealous for) and negative (i.e., be jealous or envious of) connotations. However, the word underlying "yearns jealously" in 4:5 is *phthonos*, which means "envy, jealousy." The term is unequivocally negative, referring to a vice. It therefore makes no sense to apply it to God. Rather, what James is doing in 4:5 is raising two rhetorical questions that expect a negative answer: "Do you suppose that the Scripture speaks in vain? Does the spirit which he [i.e., God] made to dwell in us crave enviously?" The Scripture in question here is Proverbs 3:34, which speaks about God's opposition to the proud and envious, and about his generous bestowal of grace on the humble.

Attributing envy to God is theologically problematic. So too is attributing temptation—understood in the sense of enticing someone to sin—to God. Pope Francis created a great stir in late 2017 when he suggested a new translation of the penultimate petition of the Our Father ("lead us not into temptation"). Francis rightly objected to the notion of God as a Father who would lead us to fall into sin; that is what Satan tries to do. The pope proposed a different translation: "Do not let us fall into temptation" (similar to French and Spanish translations). Francis certainly has the backing of James, who writes, "No one, when tempted, should say, 'I am being tempted by God'; for God cannot be tempted by evil and he himself tempts no one" (Jas 1:13).[3] Instead, God is "the Father of lights" who wants to give us what is for our good.

The preceding paragraphs about James's portrayal of God have important implications for the life of discipleship.

This is so because, in the first place, human beings are created in the divine image, "made in the likeness of God" (3:9; Gen 1:26–27). What this means, at least in part, is that human beings should reflect something of the divine goodness, to be "a kind of first fruits of his creatures" (Jas 1:18). Divine attributes like generosity, compassion, and mercy are also traits of authentic human existence. What is more, God's concern and care for the poor should inform our outlook, not least because those who suffer are God's beloved children.

Moreover, James points out that God has put into the hearts of his people "the implanted word that has the power to save your souls" (1:21). Here is another gift of our generous God, a gift to be received and welcomed with "meekness." This implanted word is a reference to God's bestowal of his law, his ways of living that reflect his holiness, in human hearts (cf. Jer 31:33). It is no accident that, a few verses later, James refers to "the law of liberty" (Jas 1:25; see also 2:12). Our covenantal God has given us the wherewithal—both the knowledge of his ways and the ability to embody them—to be his faithful people. And to live in obedience to this law is to live in true freedom, the freedom to love.

THE IMPORTANCE OF JESUS AND THE RELATIONSHIP BETWEEN FAITH AND WORKS

James refers to this law in 2:8 as "the royal law." The word translated "royal" is *basilikos*, which is from the same word group as *basileia*. The latter term is typically rendered "kingdom," and it appears throughout the Gospels of Mark, Matthew, and Luke in connection with "God" and "heaven"— that is, the "kingdom of God/heaven." Of course, it is Messiah Jesus, the Son of God, who came to inaugurate the in-breaking of God's kingdom or reign. Indeed, the first words of Jesus in

Mark's Gospel are "the time is fulfilled, and the kingdom of God has come near" (Mark 1:15). James's description of the "law of liberty" as the "royal law" can be understood as the "kingdom law," the way of living revealed by Jesus in his life and teaching.

Now, at first glance, this is a counterintuitive claim because James seems to say very little about Jesus. His name appears only twice in the entire writing: in the very first verse, where the author identifies himself as "a servant of God and of the Lord Jesus Christ" (Jas 1:1), and in 2:1, a passage to which we will return shortly. There is nothing in James's text about Jesus's life and ministry or about his saving death and resurrection. If James were the only New Testament text we had, we would learn little about Jesus. This is one of the reasons for Martin Luther's critique of the writing as "an epistle of straw." A famous advertisement campaign from years past had the punchline, "Where's the beef?" One might similarly ask, "Where's Jesus in the text?"

What comes through James's letter, however, is the *voice* of Jesus. While he never directly quotes Jesus, the text contains several allusions that evoke the latter's teaching, especially from the Sermon on the Mount (Matt 5:1—7:29). For instance, James refers to the necessity to pray to God with faith (1:6), which recalls Jesus's teaching in Matthew 7:7–8 ("Ask, and it will be given to you..."). James insists on the need to be *doers* and not just hearers of the word (1:22), which calls to mind what Jesus says in Matthew 7:24–25 ("Everyone then who hears these words of mine and acts on them..."). James calls for showing mercy (2:13) and striving for peace (3:18), which reflect two of Jesus's beatitudes ("Blessed are the merciful," Matt 5:7; "Blessed are the peacemakers," Matt 5:9). And James's admonition to avoid oaths and to let one's yes mean yes (5:12) echoes Jesus's words in Matthew 5:33–37.

Moreover, James's warning against the danger of riches (1:9) and his condemnation of exploitation by the wealthy

(2:6–7; 5:1–6) evoke Jesus's woes to the rich and satisfied in Luke 6:24–25, part of the so-called Sermon on the Plain ("But woe to you who are rich, for you have received your consolation. Woe to you who are full now, for you will be hungry"). James's statement that "the Judge is standing at the doors" (5:9) echoes Jesus's teaching in Matthew 24:33 that "he [i.e., the coming of the Son of Man] is near, at the very gates." Finally, James's teaching that love of neighbor fulfills the law (2:8; Lev 19:18) reflects what Jesus instructed (Luke 10:25–37). In short, what James proposes is an understanding of the law as interpreted and ratified by Jesus (cf. Matt 5:17–20). This is why the "law of liberty" is also the "kingdom law," the way of living in the reign of God inaugurated by Messiah Jesus. James's Christology thus draws, in large part, on Jesus as a teacher of wisdom.

But this is not the entire story. The two explicit references to Jesus name him as "Christ," that is, the Messiah (*Christos* means "anointed one") and as "Lord." The second mention of Jesus is "our *glorious* Lord Jesus Christ" (Jas 2:1), a description of Jesus as one who has been raised from the dead and exalted into heaven at God's right hand. This Lord is the one whom James expects to come again in glory (5:7–9), an expectation that Paul and others in the early Church held as well (e.g., 1 Thess 4:17). This intense expectation is a reason for dating James's work as early (e.g., in the 50s CE). So too is his use of sayings of Jesus, one that reflects an early stage of Jesus-traditions, before the Gospels were written.[4]

The reference to Jesus in 2:1 is contained within a question posed by James. The NRSV's "do you with your acts of favoritism really believe in our glorious Lord Jesus Christ?" does not, in my opinion, fully capture James's meaning. A better, more literal translation is "do you with your acts of favoritism [really] hold to the faith of Jesus Christ our glorious Lord?" The way the question is posed expects a negative answer. The "faith" or, better, the "faithfulness" (*pistis*) of Jesus points to his way of living in light of his relationship with God. This way of living is reflected, in part, in his teachings to which James alludes. We will return to the author's critique of favoritism. Demanding our attention now is the question of what constitutes authentic *pistis*.

James is adamant that faith must be expressed through works: "Faith by itself, if it has no works, is dead" (2:17). The "kingdom law" revealed and ratified by Jesus calls for loving others and showing them mercy—especially the poor and needy. In 2:14–26 James demonstrates that showing mercy involves giving aid and sustenance to those who lack adequate food and clothing (and, we can add, shelter). It is not enough just to offer words of encouragement to the naked and hungry—"Go in peace; keep warm and eat your fill" (2:16)—or to promise to pray for someone if we have the means to help. God's generosity can be experienced through the openhandedness of his people. Almsgiving is not just a pious practice; it is an authentic expression of faith. In fact, James gives a striking definition of what constitutes "pure" religion for God's covenant people: "to care for orphans and widows in their distress" (1:27)—that is, for the most vulnerable members of society.

James's essay, or mini-lecture, in 2:14–26 is famous because of later theological debates concerning the relationship between faith (*pistis*) and works (*erga*). His insistence on works in the life of faith has been taken as a counter position to Paul's teaching about the primacy of faith over works. However, to set James and Paul in opposition to one another is wrong. Paul teaches that we are justified (i.e., brought into right relationship with God) through "the faith of Jesus Christ"[5] and not by "works of the law" (Gal 2:16). The phrase "works of the law" has a technical referent—namely, Jewish practices of circumcision, dietary restrictions, and Sabbath observance.

Paul is not talking about "works" in general. In fact, he declares that "the only thing that counts is faith *working* [*energeō*, from the same root as *erga*] through love" (Gal 5:6). This is virtually the same point made by James when he says that faith, literally, "co-works" (*synergeō*), works and is brought to completion by works (Jas 2:22).

James offers two biblical examples of faith exercised through works (2:21–25). First, he raises up Abraham, whose response to God's ways culminated in his willingness to offer up his beloved son Isaac (Gen 22:1–18). James's main point here is to highlight Abraham's trust in God as the giver of life. As a "friend of God" (2:23), Abraham held nothing back from God because he realized all that he had was from God and that God could be trusted to give life, even in the face of what appeared to be a "death-dealing" situation. Moreover, given the context of showing mercy to others, James likely also has in mind Abraham's example of hospitality to the three strangers who turned out to be messengers of God (Gen 18:1–15). The notion of providing help to those in need is made explicit in James's second example, Rahab, who offered assistance and protection to the Israelite spies who were sent to reconnoiter the land (Josh 2:1–21).

FRIENDSHIP WITH GOD AND THE WISDOM FROM ABOVE

The reference to Abraham's being called God's friend leads us to the heart of James's worldview. The mini-lecture in 3:13—4:10 is a critique of those whom the author calls "double-minded" (4:8; cf. 1:8), people who claim to have friendship with God while their behavior and values show that their true friendship is "with the world" (4:4). The notion of friendship was important in the ancient world and was the topic of much writing and description (e.g., Sir 6:5–17). Typical of reflection on friendship are the following characteristics: a true friend is "another self"; friends have "one mind" (i.e., they are in basic agreement over the most important things in life); and friends share all things. The latter two certainly fit Abraham's relationship with God, as the brief description above suggests (see also, e.g., Gen 18:17–19).

Why is friendship with the world incompatible with friendship with God? Because they are grounded in two irreconcilable types of wisdom and understanding. Those who are friends of God know that God is the source of life and all blessings (Jas 1:17). They stand as *recipients* of all that they have and are. Their dignity lies in being created in God's image and likeness (3:9). They recognize that God's generosity is expansive and share his concern for and compassionate mercy toward those who suffer. God's friends are recipients of "the word of truth" (1:18) that, over time, germinates in a good life with works "done with gentleness born of wisdom" (3:13). Significantly, the word translated "gentleness" is *praútēs*, a trait associated with Jesus (Matt 11:28–29; 21:5).

The wisdom mentioned here is "the wisdom from above." James provides a beautiful description of this wisdom in 3:17. In the first place, it is "pure" (*hagnē*), signifying that it comes from God who is holy and pure; its mark on human life is innocence and holiness. The next three attributes of the wisdom from above—"peaceable, gentle, willing to yield"—produce behavior that is characterized by seeking harmonious relationships with other people, docility, and an openness to be persuaded by the truth and by the needs of others. James then lists "full of mercy and good fruits," the latter being "the fruit of righteousness" (Jas 3:18, au. trans.). Finally, this wisdom is marked by a notable absence: "without a trace of partiality or hypocrisy" (3:17). Expressed in positive terms, it produces singleness of mind and purpose, commitment to God and God's ways, as well as genuineness and integrity.

Conversely, friendship with the world derives from another type of "wisdom," one that does not even merit the name because it is "false to the truth." It "does not come down from above, but is earthly, unspiritual, devilish." James describes two characteristics of this way of thinking and being: "bitter envy and selfish ambition" (see 3:14–16). Those who are friends of the world look at life as a zero-sum game in which there are limited resources in a closed system. What is most important about life is possessing or having things, not the dignity of being. And if you have something I do not possess, it causes me pain and bitterness. I start to look at you as a competitor or, even worse, as an enemy. What motivates such a one is accumulating fortune, power, and fame. And, where this way of viewing things prevails, James observes, there is "disorder and wickedness of every kind" (3:16).

Indeed, the author goes on in 4:2 to make a startling claim: "You want something and do not have it; so you commit murder." Commit murder?!? The great Renaissance scholar Erasmus (d. 1536 CE) was so shocked at the idea of Christians killing one another that he emended the text.[6] But James is drawing here on a philosophical line of thought on the consequences of envy: killing is the outcome of envy because its "logic" stipulates that competition must be eliminated. Now, this might remain at the level of damaging relationships (e.g., regarding another as an enemy rather than as a brother or sister, one created in God's image). But such breakdown in relationships is itself a type of death. In fact, what James says in 4:2 fills out what he suggested near the beginning of the letter, that evil desire gives birth to sin, which in turn gives birth to death (1:14–15).

The root of the problem, according to James, is that the double-minded—those who claim friendship with God but instead act as friends with the world—do not adequately recognize God as the source and giver of all blessings (cf. "you do not ask"; 4:2). Or worse, they turn to God in prayer and "ask wickedly" (4:3; better than the NRSV's "ask wrongly"). That is, they pray to God "in order to spend what you get on your pleasures" or evil desires. This leads James to don the prophetic mantle and call such people "adulterers" (4:4). The Old Testament prophets used the notion of marital infidelity when chastising the people for their unfaithfulness to God (e.g., Hos 9:1). In the background here is the metaphor of marriage between God and his people, with Israel as God's bride (e.g., Jer 2:2), a beautiful image that conveys God's intimate love for his people. Similarly, the New Testament employs the imagery of the Church as the bride of Christ (e.g., 2 Cor 11:2; Eph 5:31–32).

Retaining the prophetic role, James calls the double-minded to conversion. To be friends of the world, living by its so-called wisdom, is in reality to become "an enemy of God" (Jas 4:4). James reminds the double-minded that an envious spirit is not from God (recall the discussion above concerning the translation of 4:5). He then urges them to "purify your hearts" (4:8), an apt exhortation, as the verb *hagnizō* is from the same root as the word for *pure* in 3:17, where James lists the qualities of the wisdom from above. He also calls them to humble themselves (4:10). Humility is the proper posture before God, a posture represented by open hands and a heart receptive to "the implanted word" that both enlightens and empowers the way of living that is appropriate to friendship with God.

Still donning the prophet's mantle, James follows the mini-lecture of 3:13—4:10 with a series of warnings against haughtiness in 4:11—5:6. In 4:13–17 he chastises those who arrogantly boast of future plans: "Come now, you who say, 'Today and tomorrow we will go to such and such a town and spend a year there, doing business and making money.'" The problem here is the failure to take into account God, other people and their concerns, and the fragility of life ("you are a mist that appears for a little while and then vanishes"; 4:14). This arrogant mind-set presumes that one is "God" of one's own life, fully in control and living only for oneself. But, as the friends of God know, life is a gift to be received in gratitude every day. The primary concern of God's friends is doing his will, not their own: "Thy kingdom come, thy will be done."

Then, with a voice that strongly resembles the great social prophets Amos and Isaiah, James upbraids those who live in luxury by exploiting their laborers (5:1–6). Such people live, literally, at the expense of others: "The wages of the laborers who mowed your fields, which you kept back by fraud, cry out, and the cries of the harvesters have reached the ears of the Lord of hosts" (5:4). James is unsparing and withering in his critique, not least because authentic living is more than about luxury and pleasure, both of which are ultimately ephemeral. Moreover, unlike Abraham and the friends of God, such people in their arrogance do not recognize the dignity of the poor and God's merciful love for them.

CHALLENGING AND COMFORTING EXHORTATIONS

Lest we be tempted to think, as people who do not arrogantly boast about future plans or economically exploit others, that we are excluded from James's prophetic warnings, he comes to us like Nathan the prophet. Nathan was the prophet who approached King David after the latter committed adultery with Bathsheba, impregnating her, and then arranging to have her husband, Uriah the Hittite, killed in battle. Nathan told David a story about a rich man who had a visitor to feed.

Instead of taking an animal from his many herds and flocks, he went to a poor neighbor and took and slaughtered the only animal the man owned, a precious ewe lamb. David reacted in great fury, declaring that the rich man was deserving of death and should restore the ewe lamb fourfold. Then Nathan famously pronounced to him, "You are the man!" (2 Sam 12:1–7).

James does something similar to us. In 4:11–12 he begins his warnings against arrogance by exhorting his readers not to speak evil about others or to pass judgment on their neighbors. Now, in all honesty, who of us is not guilty of doing this? "You are the person!" James makes clear why this should not be the case. God is the "one lawgiver and judge who is able to save and to destroy." Only God can look into human hearts to know what is truly going on (cf. Rom 2:16). To condemn and judge others—which we often do behind their backs—is, in effect, to play the role of God. But judgment and condemnation are God's prerogatives, not ours. To be sure, we are called to be like God by imitating his generosity and by being merciful and willing to forgive others (see Luke 6:37–38), but not by judging and condemning them.

Another way James confronts us like Nathan is through his mini-lecture on the use of speech in 3:1–12. There he opens with a comment that should give all who have the privilege to teach and preach reason to pause: they "will be judged with greater strictness" (3:1). The prior context, the mini-lecture on the necessity of works (2:14–26), gives one reason: authentic teaching and preaching must be accompanied by a corresponding way of life. Another reason becomes clear as the mini-lecture on speech develops. Words have powerful effects, and it is incumbent on teachers and preachers to use them for life-giving purposes. James observes that the power of the tongue is incommensurate with its size. To master one's tongue is to advance far along the way to spiritual maturation. He then lays out a scenario with which we are all too familiar.

The tongue with which we glorify and praise God is the same tongue with which we insult and denigrate others, people who are created in God's image. James's assessment of the double-tongued is brief and to the point: "From the same mouth come blessing and cursing. My brothers and sisters, this ought not to be so" (3:10).

What James says about the tongue can be extrapolated to the use of thumbs and fingers on various social media platforms. What damage and destruction are done through the spreading of "fake news," whether inadvertently via misinformation or deliberately via disinformation. The hurling of personal insults on public platforms is disedifying, to say the least—all the more when done by those in leadership who should be setting a good example. James's teaching about the right use of speech is a reminder that we are called to be committed to the truth, as well as to the use of all forms of communication to build up others and give them life. These are concrete ways of embodying our dignity as people made in the image of God, who created by the power of his life-giving word (Gen 1:1–31), and of being disciples of the Word made flesh, who came to reveal "the way, and the truth, and the life" (John 14:6).

James's prophetic edge is also apparent in the first mini-lecture he offers (Jas 2:1–13). This is his critique of favoritism, to which I alluded earlier in connection with his reference to holding "the faith of Jesus Christ our glorious Lord" (2:1, au. trans.). James presents a vignette, at what may have been a community gathering to settle a dispute, of superficial judgment. On the one hand, a wealthy person with gold rings and exquisite clothing is accorded much respect and the seat of honor. On the other hand, a shabbily dressed and impoverished person is literally marginalized, allowed only to stand on the sidelines. James touches a chord that resonates today: how easy it is to judge by appearances only and to be partial to what merely glitters. He once again offers a scathing critique of such judgment and shallow favoritism, and reminds his readers of *God's* perspective. God has a special love for the poor. Holding the faithfulness of Jesus involves learning to set one's mind "on divine things" rather than on "human things" (Mark 8:33).

James concludes (5:7–20) by returning to two themes with which he began, the need for endurance (1:2–4) and the importance of prayer (1:5–6). In terms of prayer, he first suggests that we should pray at all times, in good times and bad: "Are any among you suffering? They should pray. Are any cheerful? They should sing songs of praise" (5:13). The latter point ought not be passed over too quickly. It is when things are going well, when we feel great, that we can tend to forget the source of our blessings. Gratitude to God fosters and deepens our knowledge of the many ways in which God has blessed us. Moreover, it is in taking time for prayer, especially to listen to God's word, that we learn about "divine things" and take on God's values and attributes.

In addition to the prayers of individuals, James highlights the prayer of the community, especially for the sick and suffering members. He instructs, in the case of sickness, that "they should call for the elders [*presbyteroi*] of the church and have them pray over them, anointing them with oil in the name of the Lord" (5:14). This passage, along with Mark 6:13, provides the scriptural warrant for the Church's sacrament of the anointing of the sick. It is important for the sick, the suffering, and the lonely in any community of faith to be visited and to experience being *touched* by a healing hand. Moreover, in praying with and for those who suffer, we are inspired to do our part to alleviate their suffering.

James is under no illusion that the path to wisdom he proposes will be accomplished without some failures along the way. Therefore he teaches the need for honest confession of sins: "Confess your sins to one another, and pray for one another, so that you may be healed" (5:16). The final lines in the text promote what is known as fraternal correction. When we see members wandering from the path of discipleship, rather than condemn them or speak ill of them behind their backs, James encourages us to reach out in love to restore them to the community. In doing so, "you should know that whoever brings back a sinner from wandering will save the sinner's soul from death and will cover a multitude of sins" (5:20).

Admittedly, the life of discipleship set forth by James is not easy. Remember that this is a wisdom instruction, and wisdom takes time to accumulate and appropriate—not least the wisdom from above. At times, wisdom is hard earned and entails suffering. James holds up the example of "the endurance of Job" (5:11) as one who was steadfast. He also mentions the patience of farmers (5:7). The latter is a particularly apt illustration because it takes time for the implanted word to ripen and mature (1:2–4). By tending carefully to this gift—that is, by learning and being formed by the kingdom law revealed by Jesus—and by producing works of faith, we grow in heavenly wisdom and, more important, in our friendship with God.

QUESTIONS FOR PRAYER AND REFLECTION

1. Why is theology, the study of who God is and how God acts, important for all of us (and not just for academics)? What is at stake for the life of discipleship?

2. What do I make of James's insistence that God has a special love for the poor? What consoles me about it? Challenges me?

3. How does Pope Francis's observation that God as loving Father does not lead us into temptation help me to

think anew about what I am saying when I pray the Lord's Prayer?

4. In what ways does James help me to appreciate the role of Jesus as the teacher and inaugurator of the "kingdom law"?

5. How does James's insistence that faith is brought to perfection by works, especially the works of mercy, enlighten my understanding of the life of faith?

6. Why is friendship with God incompatible with friendship with the world? In what ways have I experienced the tension between them?

7. How am I being called to grow in the wisdom from above? What characteristic in the description in 3:17 most attracts me? Why?

8. How do I find myself challenged by James when he takes up the prophetic mantle?

9. In what ways does James help me to think anew about the ways I communicate to and about others?

10. How do James's exhortations about prayer—both individual and community prayer—inspire me to deepen my prayer life?

CHAPTER THREE

1 and 2 Peter (Jude)

T HE TWO LETTERS ATTRIBUTED to the apostle Peter offer material for reflection on mysteries that make up, in effect, two sides of a coin. On one side, 1 Peter teaches that Christians are on a pilgrimage to a heavenly homeland, a journey that can involve misunderstandings and hardships. Most scholars argue that the author of this text is not the apostle himself (e.g., the literary style and quality of Greek would seem beyond the ability of what we know about Peter) but instead writes in the name of Peter. I, however, am among those who see no reason why Peter is not the source of this letter, written from Rome (1 Pet 5:13; "Babylon" is code language for Rome), probably in the early 60s CE. The secretary Silvanus (5:12) may have provided the literary polish. First Peter is a circular letter to Gentile converts residing in several Roman provinces in what is present-day Turkey (1:1). These converts were experiencing opposition from their pagan neighbors. The author writes to encourage his readers, reminding them via baptismal imagery what it means to participate in the life, death, and resurrection of Jesus, the suffering servant.

On the other side of the coin, 2 Peter insists that God, who glorified his Son Jesus before eyewitnesses at the transfiguration, will be faithful in fulfilling his promises to bring about for the faithful "entry into the eternal kingdom of our Lord and Savior Jesus Christ" (2 Pet 1:11). The "day of the Lord," the return of the Lord Jesus in glory—though seemingly delayed—will come to pass (3:10) and there will be "new heavens and a new earth" (3:13). Although the author identifies himself as the apostle "Simeon Peter" (1:1) and calls this text "the second letter I am writing to you" (3:1), it contains clues that strongly suggest it is a later writing from another hand. One clue is the recognition of a *collection* of Paul's letters, now regarded as Scripture (3:15–16). A second clue is that 2 Peter draws content from the Letter of Jude,[1] a writing from the late first century CE that warns against the dangers of heeding the words and behavior of false teachers.[2] Second Peter is likely the latest New Testament text (ca. early second century CE; Peter was martyred mid-60s CE). The author of 2 Peter states that his death is imminent (1:14). Therefore, this text also functions as a farewell discourse, directed to a general audience that describes what will happen in the future, and exhorts to appropriate behavior in the present.

While 1 and 2 Peter come from different hands and times, it is still profitable to allow both letters' self-presentation as inspired by Peter's persona to guide our analysis.[3] First, I treat the letters' portrayal of Jesus as the lamb without blemish, as the Isaian suffering servant, and as shepherd. Then follows the description of the Church, largely from 1 Peter, as God's holy people by virtue of their baptism; they are "living stones" and, even more, "a royal priesthood." Next, I take up Peter's teaching about suffering and how it invites us to consider our suffering as a participation in the paschal mystery. At the end are reflections on the significance of the teaching about Jesus's second coming for the life of discipleship.

JESUS: LAMB WITHOUT BLEMISH, SUFFERING SERVANT, AND SHEPHERD

Peter describes himself as "a witness of the sufferings of Christ" (1 Pet 5:1). Early in 1 Peter, the author reminds his readers that "you were ransomed from the futile ways inherited from your ancestors, not with perishable things like silver or gold, but with the precious blood of Christ, like that of a lamb without defect or blemish" (1:18–19). A lamb without blemish evokes the story of the exodus: the Passover lamb and the splashing of its blood (after it had been sacrificed) on the doorposts and lintels (Exod 12:5–7), the blood that protected the people from the avenging angel. Indeed, it is no accident that Peter employs the metaphor of "ransom" in this connection. Just as the first Passover effected freedom from slavery in Egypt, so now Jesus's sacrifice has brought about freedom from sin and death (1 Pet 1:2—"sprinkled with his blood"). Peter's understanding is similar to that set forth in John's Gospel, where Jesus is called "the Lamb of God who takes away the sin of the world" (John 1:29).

Peter's identification of Jesus as lamb leads him to another part of Scripture, the fourth Isaian servant song (Isa 52:13—53:12).[4] Here we arrive at the most distinctive feature of 1 Peter's Christology, Jesus as the "suffering servant." First Peter 2:22–25 both quotes from and alludes to the passage from Isaiah. Verse 22 is a quotation of Isaiah 53:9: Jesus was innocent, without sin (cf. Heb 4:15), and "no deceit was found in his mouth." Like a lamb led to slaughter, he did not retaliate in the face of insult or mistreatment (1 Pet 2:23; cf. Isa 53:7). Jesus bore our sins on the cross and brought about healing through his wounds (2:24; cf. Isa 53:4–5, 12). Now, as risen Lord, Jesus is the shepherd (notice the change of metaphor from sheep to shepherd!) who gives life to those who had strayed like sheep but have turned to him for protection and guidance (2:25; cf. Isa 53:6). We will return shortly to the image of Jesus as shepherd.

This portrayal of Jesus as suffering servant functions at two levels. First, Peter reveals the salvific, efficacious quality of Jesus's suffering-unto-death through which people are led to God (see also 1 Pet 3:18, "For Christ also suffered for sins once for all, the righteous for the unrighteous, in order to bring you to God"). Second, he holds up Jesus's comportment in suffering, including his noble silence, for emulation (see 2:21, "leaving you an example"). Though he was treated unjustly, Jesus refused to strike back, to render evil for evil. He models nonviolence in action and speech, as well as the willingness to suffer for doing good while entrusting himself to God (2:23). As we will see, Peter insists that Jesus's followers are to conduct themselves as he did.

Jesus's suffering and rejection at the hands of others is contained in another scriptural image from which Peter draws, that of the rejected stone. In 1 Peter 2:7 he quotes Psalm 118:22: "The stone that the builders rejected / has become the very head of the corner." This use of stone imagery not only conveys Jesus's suffering and death, but also suggests his resurrection and vindication. Indeed, Peter insists that God "raised [Jesus] from the dead and gave him glory," with the result that our "faith and hope are set on God" (1:21). Hope is a key theme in 1 Peter, and its source is the resurrection of Jesus from the dead (1:3). Though rejected by mortals, he is the "living stone" (2:4), the cornerstone or foundation of the Church (as we will see in the next section). One characteristic of the members of the Church is that they live in hope, hope for the glory of their heavenly homeland (1:4).

As was noted above, Jesus is also the living shepherd who cares for his sheep. During his life on earth, Jesus's ministry was motivated, in large part, by his compassion for the people he encountered, who were "like sheep without a shepherd"

(Mark 6:34). He justified his ministry to sinners with the parable about a shepherd seeking out and restoring the lost sheep (Luke 15:1–7). In John's Gospel Jesus describes himself as "the good shepherd" who "lays down his life for his sheep" (John 10:1–18). Peter employs this image of Jesus the good shepherd who gave his life for straying sheep (1 Pet 2:25). Now, as risen Lord, Jesus is shepherd and "guardian" (*episkopos*, literally, "overseer," the word from which we derive "episcopal," i.e., "pertaining to bishops"). That is, Jesus *continues* to care for us, leading us to pasture and nourishment, if we but heed his voice. Peter also refers to Jesus as the "chief shepherd" (1 Pet 5:4) who will one day appear again in glory.

Jesus's coming again in glory was presaged by the event of the transfiguration, of which Peter was an eyewitness (2 Pet 1:16–18). Peter recounts the "honor and glory" received by Jesus when, from the "Majestic Glory," he heard the words, "This is my Son, by Beloved, with whom I am well pleased." In the Synoptic Gospels (e.g., Luke 9:28–36), this revelatory event occurs at the moment just before Jesus commenced his journey to Jerusalem, where he offered his life as the unblemished lamb and innocent suffering servant. In 2 Peter the recounting of this event serves to confirm the prophetic message (1:19) and to endorse Peter's role as someone who can offer an authoritative interpretation of divine revelation.

Indeed, Peter insists on the importance of Scripture in connection with his presentation of Jesus. The prophets "testified in advance to the sufferings destined for Christ and the subsequent glory" (1 Pet 1:11). We have seen one example of how the prophets testified to Jesus's sufferings, namely, Isaiah's fourth servant song. The "subsequent glory" is set forth, for example, in Daniel 7:13–14, the passage about the coming of "one like a son of man" (NRSV alt. trans.), which is evoked by the transfiguration scene. Moreover, God's word continues to be "announced to you through those who brought you the good news by the Holy Spirit sent from heaven" (1 Pet 1:12), that is, through the proclamation of the gospel. This is this "living and enduring word of God" (cf. Isa 40:8), the "imperishable seed," that brings us to new birth (1 Pet 1:23–25). God's word in Scripture, in both the Old and New Testaments, is a "lamp shining in a dark place" that Peter encourages his readers to gaze on until "the morning star rises in your hearts" (2 Pet 1:19)—until they are brought to share in the fullness of God's glory.

The divine word communicates to us "the knowledge of God and of Jesus our Lord" (2 Pet 1:2). The necessity for growth in knowledge of God and of Jesus is a leitmotif in 2 Peter (1:2–8; 2:20; 3:18). We have already touched on the exemplary manner of Jesus's endurance of suffering, which Peter holds up as essential for the life of discipleship (more on this below). In addition, 1 Peter has much to say about who God is. As the "Father of our Lord Jesus Christ," God's character is marked by "great mercy" (1:3). God is also "Father" of those who heed his call to life (1:17); as loving Father, he safeguards his children (1:5) and deeply cares for them (5:7). God bestows on them gifts to be used for building up the community of faith (4:10–11; cf. 1 Cor 12:4–7). Moreover, God is covenantal, having "chosen" a people of his own—those who heed the call of the gospel—"in order that you may proclaim the mighty acts of him who called you out of darkness into his marvelous light" (1 Pet 2:9). This God, who so chooses and calls, is "holy" (1:15), which is Peter's shorthand description for God's being and nature.

HOLY, PRIESTLY PEOPLE

God's holiness is to be reflected by his children (1 Pet 1:15–16, with a quotation from Lev 19:2) who have been "sanctified [i.e., made holy] by the Spirit" (1 Pet 1:2). First Peter has several references to baptism (e.g., 1:3, "new birth into a living hope"; 1:23, "you have been born anew"; cf. 3:21), a datum that has led some commentators to suggest that it was originally a homily or exhortation on baptism. Whether or not this is the case, it is interesting to observe that passages from this letter are proclaimed in the Church's eucharistic liturgy in Year A during the Easter season. And this is most appropriate, as Peter encourages his readers to enter more fully into the new life bestowed on them in baptism through Jesus's death and resurrection. Having died to sin, they are to "live for righteousness" (2:24; cf. Rom 6:3–5). Through God's grace, they "become participants of the divine nature" (2 Pet 1:4), a stunning expression worthy of much prayer and contemplation.

One of the striking features of 1 Peter is its ecclesiology, its description of the Church. Peter employs two metaphors that set forth the dignity and responsibility of Jesus's disciples. The first metaphor is "living stones" being built into a "spiritual house" (2:5). The cornerstone of this spiritual temple is, of course, the risen Jesus (2:4, 6). With this image, Peter reveals that, through the Holy Spirit, God dwells within his people gathered as a community of believers. While God's Spirit dwells in the hearts of the baptized (Rom 5:5), the community of faith is the sanctuary of the Spirit, as Paul also teaches: "Do you [plural, i.e., the community] not know that you are God's temple and that God's Spirit dwells in you?" (1 Cor 3:16; cf. Eph 2:19–22). It is a good practice to remind ourselves of the Spirit's presence when we are gathered for worship. So too is the recognition of the divinely bestowed dignity of our fellow "living stones."

Temples are where priests offer prayers and sacrifices. Peter's second metaphor picks up on this. The community of believers is "a holy priesthood" called "to offer spiritual sacrifices acceptable to God through Jesus Christ" (1 Pet 2:5).

Peter thereby highlights the priestly identity of *all* the baptized, an identity marker that *Lumen Gentium*, Vatican II's dogmatic constitution on the Church, emphasizes. The baptized should claim and appropriate "the common priesthood of the people." To be sure, this common priesthood does not render the ordained priesthood obsolete. The two priesthoods are ordered one to another. The baptized faithful, "by virtue of their royal priesthood, participate in the offering of the Eucharist. They exercise that priesthood, too, by the reception of the sacraments, prayer and thanksgiving, the witness of a holy life, abnegation and active charity" (*LG* 10). The list of practices in the previous sentence are a good sampling of the "spiritual sacrifices" to which Peter refers.

The phrase "royal priesthood" in the quotation from *Lumen Gentium* is taken from 1 Peter 2:9, where the author writes, "You are a chosen race, a royal priesthood, a holy nation, God's own people." The language here is from Exodus 19:6 and Isaiah 43:20–21. The former text is set at Mt. Sinai, where God entered into covenant with Israel; the latter text is contained within a passage that speaks of the renewal of this covenant. Hence, Peter suggests—similar to what we found in Hebrews and James—that the community of believers is the (new) covenant people, called to proclaim God's mighty deeds (2:9) and bear witness to the holiness of God (1:15), as noted at the outset of this section.

How do this priestly people manifest holiness? As "aliens and sojourners" (au. trans. of 1 Pet 2:11), they are to keep their eyes fixed on their heavenly inheritance that Peter significantly describes as "imperishable" (1:4). Throughout 1 Peter the author uses the terms *perishable* and *imperishable*. His readers are to focus on the second category, not the first. For example, Peter encourages them to be attentive to the genuineness of their faith, in contrast to perishable gold (1:7). He exhorts them to attend to their inner life, to the beauty of a calm, gentle character of the heart, in contrast to the ephemeral marks of beauty (e.g., hairstyles, clothing, and jewelry; see 3:4). What will assist them in developing their faith and character are "the precious blood of Christ" (1:19) and "the living and enduring word of God" (1:23)—that is, availing themselves of the imperishable gifts of the Word of God and the Eucharist.

Peter teaches that, by attending to these imperishable gifts, believers will grow in love for one another (1 Pet 4:7–8) as well as in compassion and humility (5:6). They will mature in unity, a unity that is inculcated by showing hospitality to one another (3:8; 4:9). Their reverent, chaste behavior (3:2) and blameless conduct (2:12), moreover, can function to attract outsiders to join them. Indeed, Peter seems to suggest that the best evangelizing strategy is the holy and joyful example of the faith community, which can lead any group (e.g., a religious congregation or parish) to self-examination, asking whether they comport themselves so as to attract others to join them. He also expects his readers to be ready to offer an explanation, in gentleness and reverence, to anyone who questions them about the hope that grounds their way of living (3:15–16). A good spiritual exercise is to pray and reflect on how I would respond to this question.

Second Peter 1:5–7 provides a beautiful and practical description of holiness that the priestly people are to embody. Employing the rhetorical device known as *sorites*—a chain-like construction in which the predicate of one statement forms the subject of the next (cf. Rom 5:3–4)—Peter sets forth a list of eight qualities and virtues that should distinguish Jesus's followers: faith, virtue, knowledge, self-control, steadfastness, religious devotion, brotherly (and sisterly) affection (*philadelphia*), and love. Notice how the list begins with faith and ends in love, which indicates that the life of faith should culminate in love. The point of the *sorites* is that growth in holiness depends on strengthening each one of the links of the chain.

The first three items in the list reveal that holiness entails responding to the gospel proclamation by integrating knowledge of God's ways into virtuous practices that produce a certain "character," the mental and moral qualities that make Christians distinctive. In other words, Peter is talking about character formation (cf. 1 Pet 3:4). The last three items make clear a point on which Jesus insisted, namely, that love of God (i.e., our religious devotion and piety) and love of neighbor go hand in hand (Mark 12:28–34 and par.). "Love" (*agapē*), the crowning jewel of the list, expresses both aspects, and this love is possible only because of God's love revealed through the good news concerning Jesus. The two items in the middle—self-control and steadfastness—show the importance of discipline and faithful endurance in the life of faith. Spiritual discipline and perseverance are appropriate lifelong responses to the new life God has bestowed on us in baptism. They are aided by *hope*, which, though it remains only implicit in the *sorites*, is part of the program for maturation in holiness as presented by Peter.

Peter concludes this list with two inferences that follow "if these things [i.e., the list of eight qualities] are yours and are increasing among you" (2 Pet 1:8). One inference is that his readers will confirm their call and election from God (1:10), which, as we have seen, is to be a holy, priestly people. In addition, they will show that their "knowledge of our Lord Jesus Christ" is bearing fruit (1:8). Recall that, in 1 Peter, Jesus the suffering servant is held up as an example for the community of faith to emulate. It is to this aspect of Peter's teaching that we now turn, one that requires nuance and care.

PARTICIPATION IN THE PASCHAL MYSTERY[5]

Suffering is a recurrent theme in 1 Peter. The author refers to the suffering of the letter's recipients in different ways: they are being maligned as evildoers (2:12); they are enduring pain while suffering unjustly (2:19); they are abused for their "good conduct in Christ" (3:16). The first and third descriptions intimate a context of new Christians whose friends and those with whom they associated prior to their conversion now oppose them because of their change in values and lifestyle. The second description alludes to the situation whereby some community members who were slaves were being maltreated by their masters.

Peter's instructions to the maltreated slaves needs careful interpretation: "If you endure when you do right and suffer for it, you have God's approval" (2:20). It is at this point in the letter that the author inserts the example of Jesus as the suffering servant (2:21–25). It is crucially important to emphasize that the institution of slavery, a reality in which one person is owned by another as "property," does not fit our present context (though, tragically, some people are caught up in various forms of "trafficking" that leave them in an enslaved condition). This text should never to be used to justify abuse of vulnerable persons, nor applied to encourage someone to remain in an abusive relationship or situation. The suffering caused by abuse—whether it be physical, emotional, or psychological—should be confronted and the victim be rescued from it. This is not to say that, in their healing, victims of abuse cannot take comfort in knowing that Jesus also suffered unjustly and can empathize with their pain.

There *is* suffering, however, that happens as a result of Christian commitment (as noted in chapter 1). Peter refers to this as suffering "as a Christian" (4:16). There are places around the globe where Christians are persecuted for the very reason that they are Christians. Moreover, Christian values can and do rub up against the social and political mores in contemporary situations and contexts. To stand up and advocate for those values (e.g., the right to life from conception to natural death;

human rights of refugees and immigrants; racial justice; economic and ecological justice) can lead to the heaping of scorn and derision on one's head. To be a Christian can also entail putting up with "scoffers" (2 Pet 3:3), those who mock the faith and its adherents. It is in this context of suffering for the sake of Jesus and his gospel that Peter's use of the example of the suffering servant is relevant.

As noted above, the depiction of Jesus as suffering servant functions, at one level, to hold up his nonretaliation as an example to follow. This echoes the challenging teaching of Jesus in the Sermon on the Mount: "If anyone strikes you on the right cheek, turn the other also" (Matt 5:39). Jesus's way is nonviolent resistance. In the same sermon, Jesus goes on to instruct his followers to "love your enemies and pray for those who persecute you" (Matt 5:44). Peter exhorts his audience in a similar manner: "Do not repay evil for evil or abuse for abuse; but, on the contrary, repay with a blessing" (1 Pet 3:9). To be sure, what is proposed here is among the most difficult, if not *the* hardest, of Jesus's teachings to follow. It is also what makes (or, at least, should make) Christianity so radical. We must remember that Christ "suffered for sins once for all, the righteous for the unrighteous, in order to bring you to God" (3:18).

This brings us to another level of the presentation of Jesus as suffering servant. In his life and ministry, Jesus encountered much suffering—including misunderstanding, opposition from religious leaders, the failure of his disciples (at times) to comprehend him and his teachings, abandonment by friends and disciples, and most of all, the terrible ignominy and agony of the crucifixion. It is essential to appreciate that Jesus's sufferings were *consequential* to his fidelity to his fundamental vocation to reveal God's love (see John 3:16; 13:1). That is, in the course of his ministry of teaching, feeding, healing, and reaching out to sinners, Jesus evoked much opposition. Thus, his suffering was not suffering for the sake of suffering itself but was a result of doing what God called him to do in inaugurating God's kingdom. To be sure, Jesus came to embrace this destiny, setting his face resolutely to go to Jerusalem (Luke 9:51) and praying to the Father on the night before he died, "not what I want, but what you want" (Mark 14:36).

According to Isaiah, the life of the suffering servant, the "righteous one," was an "offering for sin." He "bore the sin of many" and through his suffering "shall make many righteous" (Isa 53:10–13). Peter—along with many New Testament writers, not to mention Jesus himself (e.g., Mark 10:45)—interpreted Christ's life, suffering, and death via the Isaian servant. Jesus "suffered for sins once for all" in order to bring us to God (1 Pet 3:18). We have been ransomed from sin and death by "the precious blood of Christ" (1:19), our sins forgiven as we have been "sprinkled with his blood" (1:2). Moreover, God vindicated Jesus's revelation of divine love—even to the point of giving his life—by raising him from the dead. Ascended and seated at God's right hand (3:18), he has paved the way to eternal life.

What Peter sets forth here is known today as "the paschal mystery." This phrase refers to Christ's "passing over" to the Father through his passion, death, resurrection, and ascension. This mystery speaks to the power of God, manifested through his Son, to bring life out of death, to effect redemption and salvation through suffering, to bring joy and peace out of suffering and pain. The paschal mystery thereby entails *redemptive suffering*. Through the outpouring of the Holy Spirit, we too can participate in this great mystery. Indeed, we are *called* to participate (as evident in the liturgies of the Easter Triduum). Here's where 1 Peter offers a helpful—and hopeful—message for those who are suffering. And not just for those who suffer in the ways mentioned above (though, surely, they are included), but also for those whose sufferings are part and parcel of being human.

To be human is to suffer, and suffering can take various forms: loneliness, loss of job, economic insecurity, chronic pain and/or illness, broken relationships, grieving the loss of loved ones, to mention some. Suffering can turn us in on ourselves. For some people, suffering can become so severe that taking one's own life seems a better option than to continue living with the pain. But our suffering can take on meaning and significance when we offer it in union with Jesus's redemptive suffering. Some versions of morning offering prayers include the offering of one's sufferings with Jesus's salvific suffering. Since my illness (see note 5), I have been attracted to the Prayer of Surrender by the Jesuit Walter Ciszek.[6] In it, he offered the sadness in his heart "in union with your [Jesus's] sufferings, for those who are in deepest need of your redeeming grace." Notice his conviction about the *ongoing* outworking of the paschal mystery. Fr. Ciszek's prayer also calls for surrendering in trust to God's will, in imitation of Jesus. Such surrender is an expression of trust in God, who brings life out of death, and is a confession of *hope*. Peter captures this dynamic as follows: "Rejoice insofar as you are sharing Christ's sufferings, so that you may also be glad and shout for joy when his glory is revealed" (1 Pet 4:13).

SIGNIFICANCE OF THE SECOND COMING OF JESUS IN GLORY

Peter was not only "a witness of the sufferings of Christ"; he also insists that he "shares in the glory to be revealed" (1 Pet 5:1). In terms of the latter, Peter recounts how he was one of the "eyewitnesses of his [i.e., Jesus's] majesty," the majesty disclosed at his transfiguration (2 Pet 1:16–18). This mysterious event reveals many things about Jesus, including its being a "preview" to his apostles of the glory that awaited him following his journey to Jerusalem that led to the cross. This notice of Jesus's glory sets the stage for 2 Peter's teaching about the coming of the Lord in glory—that is, "the coming of the day of God" (3:12)—in the final chapter of the letter.

The reason Peter insists on this point is to rebut the "scoffing" of certain skeptics (3:3). He gives voice to their scoffing: "Where is the promise of his [i.e., Christ's] coming? For ever since our ancestors died, all things continue as they were from the beginning of creation!" (3:4). The New Testament gives evidence that early Christians expected the *parousia*—the glorious return of the risen Lord Jesus at the end of history—to happen very soon.[7] By the time of the writing of 2 Peter, several decades had passed. The scoffers were mocking Christian belief, as it came to be expressed in the Nicene Creed, that "he [i.e., the risen Jesus] will come again in glory to judge the living and the dead."

This skepticism was not merely about theological niceties. The scoffing contained dangerous implications, and Peter was keenly aware of them. One was the denial of the basis of Christian hope, namely, "the resurrection of the dead and the life of the world to come" (Nicene Creed) to be ushered in by the *parousia*. The scoffers also called into question whether history is moving toward a definitive goal. Doesn't human experience show instead that history is an endless repetition of cycles (cf. Eccl 1:9)? Isn't Christian hope and expectation for God's ultimate intervention to bring about new heavens and a new earth mere folly? Notice that behind the scoffing is the denial of God's involvement in the world and of God's leading history to its culmination in the full manifestation of God's reign.

Peter responds to the skepticism with fiery passion. He refers to the story of the flood (Gen 6:5—9:17) to illustrate how God brought judgment upon sinful humanity (2 Pet 3:5-6).

While this reference serves as a warning to the scoffers of the judgment to come (3:7), the reference to Genesis also functions to argue that the world is the result of God's creative word and that creation is dependent on God's power to remain in existence. The world is more than random chance. God is involved in the world. What remains unsaid is that God's involvement in the world has been revealed most dramatically through the coming of Jesus as a human being and through the outpouring of the Spirit.

God's involvement with the world means that God is involved in history. The "day of the Lord" will come, at which point history will reach its culmination (2 Pet 3:10). Peter insists that God's timetable is different from ours: "With the Lord one day is like a thousand years, and a thousand years are like one day" (3:8). God is the ruler of creation and history. What might seem like a long "delay" is in reality a manifestation of God's patience and forbearance. In his love for humanity, God does not desire that people die in their sins; rather, God wants "all to come to repentance" (3:9), including the scoffers. Notice that word *all*. As is stated in 1 Timothy 2:4, God "desires everyone to be saved and to come to the knowledge of the truth."

What do we make of Peter's insistence that the risen Lord will come again in glory at the end of time? Here we are, nearly two thousand years later, and we are still waiting. First, it's important to recall Peter's teaching that God's time is not our time. We are keenly aware that some groups of Christians have been obsessed with determining the precise date of Jesus's coming in glory, often with disastrous consequences. It's helpful to recall Jesus's words in Mark 13:32: "About that day or hour no one knows, neither the angels in heaven, nor the Son, but only the Father."

Most Christians are not obsessed with ascertaining the time of the *parousia*. But we do well to keep near the forefront of our minds our belief in the Lord's coming again in glory. Indeed, the season of Advent is an annual reminder of the importance of this belief for the life of the Church. The one whose coming in the flesh we celebrate at Christmas is the one for whom we await to return in glory. We daily pray to the Father, "Thy kingdom come"—that is, that God's reign come in its fullness. How often do I allow this hope and expectation to inform my outlook? Do I long for the coming of the Lord?

The *parousia* is the horizon toward which history is moving. The best way to wait for the Lord is to commit myself, each and every day, to allow God to work through me so that his kingdom be realized more and more on earth as it is in heaven. The celebration of Advent also encourages us to look at the shortness of life. For most of us, our moment of death will be our experience of the coming of the Lord, as we appear before him who embodies mercy and compassion. We do well to live each day with the awareness of life's brevity—not out of a cowering fear, but in joyful hope as we trod the path of holiness set forth in the *sorites* of 2 Peter 1:5–7. What is the end of such a way of life? "When the chief shepherd appears, you will win the crown of glory that never fades away" (1 Pet 5:4).

This path of holiness is not just an individual journey but is done with others. Recall Peter's image of living stones "built into a spiritual house, to be a holy priesthood, to offer spiritual sacrifices acceptable to God through Jesus Christ" (2:5). This spiritual house has as its cornerstone the one who, as suffering servant, revealed the way of nonretaliation. His suffering and death—and resurrection and glorification—are the means through which the God of life has brought about the forgiveness of sins and eternal life. We can unite our sufferings with the redemptive sufferings of Christ as we wait in joyful hope for his coming again in glory.

QUESTIONS FOR PRAYER AND REFLECTION

1. What do I find challenging about 1 Peter's portrayal of Jesus through the figure of the Isaian suffering servant? What is consoling about this image?

2. Why is it important to appreciate that Jesus's sufferings were in consequence of his fidelity to his fundamental vocation to reveal God's love?

3. Which of Peter's images of the Church do I find most inspiring? Why?

4. How have I exercised my priestly calling and identity as part of God's priestly people? How is God inviting me to appropriate even more this identity?

5. How does the *sorites* in 2 Peter 1:5–7 speak to me about formation in Christian character and in the way to holiness?

6. What sufferings in my life do I find most challenging and difficult? How might offering those sufferings in union with Jesus's redemptive suffering change my way of thinking about them?

7. Peter talks about suffering "as a Christian" (i.e., the suffering that comes to those whose Christian convictions and values are opposed). When and how have I experienced this type of suffering? If I haven't undergone such suffering, what might that say about my witness to the gospel?

8. How conscious am I of God's involvement in the world and in history? How have I experienced God's presence and involvement in my life?

9. What comes to mind when I think of the return of the Lord in glory and of judgment?

10. How might I appreciate better the season of Advent and its emphasis on the second coming of Jesus? How would I respond to someone who asked me to give an account of my hope (1 Pet 3:15)?

CHAPTER FOUR

1, 2, and 3 John

THE THREE LETTERS attributed to "John" are descendants of the Fourth Gospel. That is, they are products of the community of faith that found its inspiration in the Beloved Disciple, the key source for that Gospel (John 21:24). These letters employ several symbols and motifs found in John's Gospel, such as the themes of God's love and the eternal life bestowed through Christ, the contrast between light and darkness, the emphasis on truth, and the opposition of the "world."

The author of 2 and 3 John identifies himself as "the Elder" (*presbyteros*, from which we get *presbyter* and *presbyteral*), one of the leaders of a network of communities grounded in the Johannine tradition. There is no identification of the author of 1 John, which is presented as coming from more than one person (the pronoun *we* permeates this writing). Nevertheless, there is a definite kindred spirit among these writings, and most scholars argue that they come from the same source.[1] The date and provenance of these writings are hard to ascertain. In terms of the former, a good estimate is the end of the first century CE.

What precisely are these writings and what is their relationship with one another? Third John is a personal letter written to a man named Gaius, who likely was the host of a house church in the Johannine network of communities. This short letter (think postcard) commends a certain Demetrius, who was likely the one who delivered it (3 John 12). Second John is another short letter written to a house church (the referent of "elect lady"; 2 John 1), probably the church that met in Gaius's house. This letter was to be read to the entire community. First John is not a letter per se (i.e., it lacks standard epistolary features, such as identification of the sender and the addressee, greetings at the end, etc.). It reads more like a homiletic treatise. The best explanation of their relationship is that these texts originally formed a three-letter "packet." Demetrius delivered a letter from the Elder to Gaius (3 John). He also brought a letter to be read to the assembly (2 John), as well as a more general homiletic discourse that was intended to be read not only in Gaius's house church but also in other house churches in the network. We might think of 1 John as a circular letter.

More important than determining these critical background issues is presenting the content these writings set forth, the focus of this chapter. First, I treat the beautifully simple statement in 1 John that "God is love" as revealed through Jesus, the incarnate Son of the Father. Then comes the portrayal of the Church as the family of faith, with the Elder's emphasis on *koinōnia* ("fellowship," "communion") as its distinguishing characteristic. Next, I wrestle with some paradoxes and puzzles these texts present. Finally, I look at the splintering of the Johannine community and reflect on ways these writings suggest for maintaining *koinōnia* in the Church.

"GOD IS LOVE," REVEALED THROUGH JESUS THE INCARNATE SON

Grammatically, the simplest sentence form is "X is Y." The subject (X) is linked ("to be" is a linking verb) to a predicate

(Y), either a noun or an adjective. The predicate functions to give a definition and/or description of the subject. In the New Testament, there are only two examples of this form of sentence that has *God* as the subject, and both are found in 1 John. Who or what, according to the Elder, is God? First and foremost, "God is *love* [*agape*]" (1 John 4:8, 16). This simple expression describes the identity and very nature of God. Love is who God is and what God does. And what God did was this: "God sent his only Son into the world so that we might live through him" (4:9). This echoes what the Fourth Gospel famously proclaims: "God so loved the world that he gave his only Son, so that everyone who believes in him may not perish but may have eternal life" (John 3:16).

Let's not allow our familiarity with these words to lead us to pass over them too quickly. A couple of observations. First, the image of God giving his only Son to us communicates that God holds nothing back in expressing his love for us (something parents of an only child can especially appreciate). Notice, too, how God's love is expressed in his intention to bestow *life*. This leads us to the second of the Elder's "God is Y" statements: "God is *light*" (1 John 1:5). Think of the importance of sunlight for giving us life. Sunlight not only enables us to find our way around and to receive warmth. It is also an energy source, making possible the production of oxygen by plants. Light is an apt symbol of God's dynamic life-creating power, the power that is rooted in love. The life that God gives through Christ, moreover, includes the forgiveness of sins: "In this is love…[God] loved us and sent his Son to be an expiation for our sins" (au. trans. of 4:10). The life God bestows is more than our physical existence, though it surely includes that. This life is *eternal* life (5:11).

The fact of the incarnation of Jesus reveals the great "divine condescension." God so desired, in love, to reveal himself to us that he became one of us. Think of an adult who bends down to a child and speaks lovingly in simple terms so that the child can appreciate what is being communicated. The Elder refers to the incarnation at the very outset of 1 John, thus underlining its importance: "We declare to you what was from the beginning, what we have heard, what we have seen with our eyes, what we have looked at and touched with our hands, concerning the word of life" (1:1).[2] As we will see, the Johannine epistles repeatedly insist on the importance of Jesus's humanity. As "the word of life," he is the very self-expression of God, the one who can reveal who God is because he himself is God, through whom the Father creates and bestows life (John 1:1–18).[3]

That the Word became flesh and dwelt among us (John 1:14) does not, however, tell the whole story. Jesus most eloquently revealed God's love by giving his life for us: "We know love by this, that he [i.e., Jesus] laid down his life for us" (1 John 3:16). Just as the Father holds nothing back from us in sending his Son, so Jesus held nothing back—not even his life—in revealing God's love. Indeed, he proclaimed in John's Gospel, "No one has greater love than this, to lay down one's life for one's friends" (15:13).

For now, it is crucial to appreciate Jesus's revelation of God's love, the *agapē* that is expressed through self-giving so that others may have life. At the beginning of his passion account, the evangelist John expressed it this way: "Jesus knew that his hour had come to depart from this world and go to the Father. Having loved his own who were in the world, he loved them to the end" (13:1). The phrase "to the end" translates the Greek *eis telos*, which signifies not only that Jesus loved his followers to the very "end" of his life but also to "the full extent"—that is, with the offering of his life.

The Elder emphasizes the life-giving effects of Jesus's self-gift in love, especially the forgiveness of sins. He refers to Jesus's death as "expiation for our sins" (auth. trans. of 1 John 4:10) "and not for ours only but also for the sins of the whole world" (2:2). God's revelation of life-giving love is truly expansive; there are no limits! The Elder highlights "the blood of Jesus" that cleanses from all sin (1:7).

Why this focus on Jesus's blood? While the situation in the Johannine communities that lies behind the texts is difficult to reconstruct with precision, there were apparently some people who downplayed—perhaps even denied—the humanity of Jesus. In 1 John 2:18–19 the Elder refers to a group that has left the community. He calls them "antichrists," a term that points to people who have a wrong understanding of who Jesus is. In 2 John 7 he calls "antichrist" a group of people "who do not confess that Jesus Christ has come in the flesh." It is not clear to us today why some community members (at least former ones) played down Jesus's humanity. My guess is that they may have been scandalized by a crucified Messiah, and thus their emphasis was solely on the Spirit-filled Jesus who, following his baptism, performed mighty deeds and wonders.

In any event, the Elder insists that "this is the one who came by water and blood, Jesus Christ, not with the water only but with the water and the blood" (1 John 5:6). Recall that, in John's Gospel, after Jesus had died on the cross, a soldier lanced his side with a spear, and "at once blood and water came out" (John 19:34). The Elder is thus adamant that Jesus was human and that he gave his life on the cross. Once again, Jesus's self-giving death is the epitome of the revelation of God's love. Moreover, the life-giving effects of this love are experienced in the sacraments of baptism and the Eucharist, symbolized by the blood and water flowing from the crucified Jesus's side.

We do well to reflect often on the mystery of the cross. Crucifixes adorn our churches (at least in the Catholic tradition). Many people have a crucifix hung in a prominent place in their home. And many wear a crucifix on a chain or necklace. These are pious practices. We may ask ourselves, however, how often do I pause and reflect on what is represented by the crucifix I pass by or put on and wear? It should never become mere decoration or ornamentation. The salutary spiritual exercise of the Stations of the Cross—especially during the season of Lent—reminds us of the love of God revealed through Jesus in his death on the cross. As Paul expressed it, "Christ loved us and gave himself up for us, a fragrant offering and sacrifice to God" (Eph 5:2).

God's love is also revealed in the bestowal of the Holy Spirit. As is the case with John's Gospel, the verb *abide* (*menō*) is prominent in 1 John. Specifically, the themes of our abiding or remaining in God and God's (and Jesus's) abiding in us pervade the text. To abide in Jesus, as branches on the vine, is the way to true life and to the empowerment to bear the fruit of good works (John 15:1–11). The Elder reminds his readers that "by this we know that [God] abides in us, by the Spirit that he has given us" (1 John 3:24; cf. 4:13).

Observe that the Holy Spirit is a *gift*. Through the Spirit, God deigns to dwell in us as individuals, another manifestation of God's desire in love to draw close to us. God not only took on flesh in the person of Jesus two thousand years ago. God's presence *continues*, and in a more pervasive way than in the time of Jesus (i.e., as a man he was limited in time and place). This mystery is behind Jesus's words at the Last Supper: "Nevertheless I tell you the truth: it is to your advantage that I go away, for if I do not go away, the Advocate [i.e., the Holy Spirit] will not come to you; but if I go, I will send him to you" (John 16:7). This Spirit is God's love poured into our hearts (1 John 4:16; cf. Rom 5:5). Prayerful meditation on this mystery of divine love can never be fully exhausted.

THE FAMILY OF FAITH AND *KOINŌNIA*

The Elder has more to say about the gift of the Spirit. This gift is an "anointing" (1 John 2:20, 27; likely a reference to baptism) that makes its recipients children of God. The Elder stands in awe of this expression of God's love: "See what love the Father has given us, that we should be called children of God; and that is what we are" (3:1). Those "who have been born of God" are empowered "because God's seed abides in them" (3:9). There's that word "abide" again! Even more striking is the image of God's "seed" (*sperma*) indwelling us. The imagery suggests two things. First, this indwelling seed will enable a process of growth and maturation. Second, because this seed is the Spirit, the divine dynamism within us, that growth and maturation entail taking on the "family likeness" of God, whose children we are.

More specifically, the Spirit-empowered growth and maturation involves manifesting a particular pattern of living, the pattern of self-giving love. Throughout 1 John, the Elder writes of God's love being "perfected" and "brought to completion" (au. trans. of 2:5; see also 4:12, 17) in us. The verb here is *teleioō*, which indicates movement toward a goal—in this instance, eternal life in the presence of God along with all God's children, transformed to "be like him, for we will see him as he is" (3:2). To this end, the Spirit confers the gift of knowledge (2:20), the knowledge about Jesus and how he revealed God's love, most dramatically in the foot washing scene at the Last Supper (John 13:1–20). That the incarnate Jesus is the pattern for God's children to take on the "family likeness" is another reason why the Elder insists on the importance of his humanity.

The Elder keeps things simple when it comes to setting forth the "commandment" of God (though this is not the same as saying it's easy!): "that we should believe in the name of his

Son Jesus Christ and love one another, just as he [i.e., Jesus] has commanded us" (1 John 3:23). To believe in Christ is to accept that Jesus, the incarnate Word of God, is the definitive revelation of God's love. It is to open our minds and hearts to Christ as the Bread of Life (John 6:35–51), the one who gives us true nourishment and life. It is to grow in the transformative knowledge of Jesus, who though Lord and Master, set the "example" or "pattern" (*hypodeigma*; John 13:15) of humble, tender, self-giving love when he washed his disciples' feet.

Jesus's command to his disciples to love one another as he has loved them followed immediately upon this scene (John 13:34). This is the "new commandment" to which the Elder refers in 1 John 2:8. Simply put, they are "to walk just as he [i.e., Jesus] walked" (2:6). The verb translated "walk" is *peripateō*, which has the broader sense of "comporting oneself" and "living as a habit of conduct."

As I intimated, this sounds so simple, but it is not easy. It is crucial to recall that this love originates with God. It is not self-generated but rather is a gift to be received and lived. "We love because [God] first loved us" (4:19). We can only give to others what we have first received. Prayer, both personal and communal, and the regular reception of the sacraments—especially the Eucharist—inculcate the reception of God's love. Like Peter when Jesus came to wash his feet, we may at times not feel ourselves worthy of such a gift (John 13:6–8). Love does not coerce or force its way on another. Jesus is always there, smile on his face, towel around his waist, waiting for us to receive his gift of love if we but open ourselves to it.

The Elder puts his finger on another challenge that this teaching about love involves. It is often easier to love the one who is not seen (i.e., God) than to love those whom we do see around us—including family members, members of a religious community, work associates, and so on. People close to us can, at times, grate on us. Habits and mannerisms of others, sometimes of those who are closest to us, can wear us down. The Elder, however, reminds us that this must not be so in the family of God: "Those who say, 'I love God,' and hate their brothers and sisters, are liars; for those who do not love a brother or sister whom they have seen, cannot love God whom they have not seen....Those who love God must love their brothers and sisters also" (1 John 4:20–21).

Such love calls forth the virtues of patience, tolerance, and forbearance. It also helps to be humble, to know that I at times can make it difficult for others to love me. Jesus's love command, the way of love he embodied and empowers, should find its implementation and practice—in the first place—among those around us, whom we literally see much of the time. The Elder would concur wholeheartedly with the maxim "charity begins at home." The result of such love is true "fellowship" or "communion" (*koinōnia*). Here we arrive at a crucially important theme in 1 John, signaled by its appearance in the opening lines: "We declare to you what we have seen and heard so that you also may have fellowship with us; and truly our fellowship is with the Father and his Son Jesus Christ" (1:3; cf. 1:7). Abiding in God and his Son also means abiding in love with the family of faith.

For the Elder, *koinōnia* is both a gift and a task. Recall that Jesus, in his prayer at the Last Supper, prayed that the family of faith "may all be one. As you, Father, are in me and I am in you, may they also be in us" (John 17:21). It is crucially important to appreciate Jesus's reason for such unity: "so that the world may believe that you have sent me" (17:21). That is, the *koinōnia* of the family of faith—in religious and parish communities, in the Catholic Church, and more broadly among the Christian churches—bears witness to the power of God's love as revealed through Jesus. The realization of *koinōnia* is thus a vital means of evangelization.[4] Communities of faith do well to reflect on whether the following words of Jesus describe them: "By this everyone will know that you are my disciples, if you have love for one another" (13:35).

The Elder offers his readers another way to participate in the work of evangelization. They can do so by offering hospitality and material support to those who proclaim the gospel (3 John 5–8). In his day, traveling missionaries relied on such hospitality and support in the network of house churches. In our time, that support is typically expressed by financial contributions for those who carry on the work of the gospel in places near and far. Through such support, those who give generously "become co-workers" (v. 8) in the proclamation of the gospel. This support is also another expression of the Church's *koinōnia*, as well as a way of showing love for people whom we do not see (e.g., in mission lands).

Mention of people whom we do not see leads to a last point in this section. I refer here to those people in our midst, such as the poor and homeless, whom we can at times prefer not to notice. How easy it is to avert our eyes when we see someone in need. The Elder issues a challenging warning to us: "How does God's love abide in anyone who has the world's goods and sees a brother or sister in need and yet refuses help?" (1 John 3:17; cf. Jas 2:14–26). The family of faith, whose members' distinguishing characteristic is the self-giving love of God revealed in Jesus's foot washing love, is to bear witness to that love via compassionate outreach to the distressed and marginalized. By doing so, they bear eloquent witness to the gospel.

PARADOXES AND PUZZLES

While much in the Johannine letters seems straightforward, these texts also present some paradoxes and puzzles. I alluded to one of those in the previous section when I mentioned the Elder's writing "a new commandment" to the community

(1 John 2:8). In the immediately preceding verse, however, he states, "Beloved, I am writing you no new commandment, but an old commandment that you have had from the beginning; the old commandment is the word that you have heard" (2:7). So which is it? An old or new commandment? What is going on here?

To answer these questions, we need to go first to John's Gospel. At the Last Supper, after washing his disciples' feet, Jesus declares to them, "I give you a new commandment, that you love one another" (13:34a). Now, the commandment to love is from one perspective "old," since it was commanded in the Old Testament (cf. Deut 6:4–5, to love God with your whole being; and Lev 19:18, "you shall love your neighbor as yourself"). Jesus himself refers to these two love commandments in his response to the question about which commandment is greatest (see Mark 12:28–34 and par.). What makes Jesus's commandment at the Last Supper "new" is that his foot washing love is the exemplar of self-giving love. Indeed, after introducing the phrase "new commandment," Jesus instructs his disciples, "Just as I have loved you, you also should love one another" (John 13:34b). The "just as" is the model he has just shown to them. Moreover, through the gift of the Spirit, his followers are now empowered to embody this way of love. That is, what is "new" is what is called *imitatio Christi*, embodying in our lives the love of Jesus.

Returning to 1 John, the "old commandment" now refers to the commandment to love as Jesus loved. This is what the community learned when the gospel was first preached to them: "the old commandment is the word that you have heard" (1 John 2:7). But this commandment is still "new" in the sense that it is "new" in John's Gospel (as just explained), including the fact that the outpouring of the Spirit has created the possibility in the Johannine community of this new way of "walking": "the darkness is passing away and the true light is already shining" (2:8). The Elder calls them to bear witness to what Paul calls life in the "new creation" (cf. 2 Cor 5:17).

A more perplexing paradox revolves around the issue of sin. On the one hand, the Elder states, "If we say that we have no sin, we deceive ourselves, and the truth is not in us" (1 John 1:8; for more, see 1:5—2:6). On the other hand, he claims, "Those who have been born of God do not sin, because God's seed abides in them; they cannot sin, because they have been born of God" (3:9; see also 3:4–10 and 5:18). This latter claim can disturb, because who of us can honestly say, "I have not sinned"? And if that is so, am I disqualified from my identity as a child of God? How do we reconcile this apparent discrepancy, the simultaneous claims that we are all guilty of sin and that Christians, members of God's family, do not—indeed, *cannot*—sin?

One way to understand this tension is to think in terms of the "already but not yet" quality of Christian existence. The reality of sin exists, and each one of us sins on occasion. The reason the Elder insists on this reality—in addition to its evident truth—is that Jesus is the expiation of our sins (4:10) and of those of the whole world (2:2). Each one of us stands in need of salvation. Moreover, the Elder exhorts the community to pray for a brother or sister who is committing sin (one that is not "mortal") in order that God give life to such a one (5:16). In short, the Elder is keenly aware of the reality of sin and of members of the community failing at times, and that they have need of confession and forgiveness. Sinlessness awaits the future.

And yet, the Elder is even more sanguine about what God has *already* accomplished through Jesus and about what he *will* bring to completion in the future. God has won the victory over the evil one (cf. 3:8b). For this reason, he can say that God's children have been forgiven (2:12). Even more, in their future state—when they will see God face-to-face (3:1-2)—they will be so transformed that sin is no longer possible. As recipients of the gift of the Spirit, through whom they abide in God and in Christ, their maturation toward perfection (recall the comments above about the verb *teleioō*) involves allowing the promised goal of being in God's presence and becoming like him to inform more and more their behavior and character development in the present: "all who have this hope in [God] purify themselves, just as he is pure" (3:3).

Another puzzling aspect of 1 John pertains to his teaching about prayer. The Elder, in discussing the "boldness" God's children can have before him, writes, "We receive from him whatever we ask, because we obey his commandments and do what pleases him" (3:22). Is it our experience that we always receive from God "whatever we ask"? Many people pray longingly and fervently for intentions like the healing of a loved one. Nevertheless, such prayers often seem to go unheeded. Is the Elder overly confident in the power of prayer? Before addressing this question, it is important to dispel a possible misunderstanding of what is said in the words quoted above. They could be construed as suggesting that, *if* we obey God, then he will answer our prayers. But that is not the direction of causality the Elder intends.

His meaning is better captured by what he writes in 1 John 5:14: "And this is the boldness we have in him [i.e., God], that if we ask anything according to his will, he hears us." The key phrase here is *according to God's will*. A mark of maturity in the life of prayer is, first and foremost, to *listen* to God. In listening to God, we grow in the ability to discern the divine will for us—as well as be inspired and strengthened to obey it in our lives. Obedience to God is the *fruit* of prayer.[5] As alluded to in the previous chapter, Jesus exemplified this way of praying when, in the garden on the night before he died, he prayed to God his loving *Abba*, "Not what I want, but what you want" (Mark 14:36). When we pray in the spirit of "thy kingdom come, thy will be done"—and commit ourselves to discerning God's will in our lives and to putting it into practice—we can be assured that our prayer will be answered.

A final puzzlement on which to comment is the Elder's manner of presentation. His style of teaching is characterized more by repetition (and, admittedly, some circularity) than by logical argumentation. That's not to say that he lacks lucidity. In fact, his main point concerning love is exemplary in its clarity. As we have seen, our ability to love is grounded in the fact that God "first loved us" (1 John 4:19; cf. 4:16). God's love, especially as revealed in Jesus, is the source of any love we can express—both for God and for one another.

Speaking of love, the Elder famously observes, "There is no fear in love, but perfect love casts out fear" (4:18). As he goes on to comment, fear pertains to punishment. Admittedly, to conduct oneself so as to avoid being punished can keep one out of trouble. But vis-à-vis our relationship with God and with others, the Elder teaches that love in the sense of *agapē* is the most noble motivation and driving force, what leads to "perfection." To say that there is no fear in love does not deny the importance of "fear of the Lord" in the life of discipleship. The latter refers to the awe with which we should always regard God who is love and light. In this respect, what we fear is offending such a loving God. True fear of the Lord is consistent with the Elder's teaching. Indeed, it is the appropriate stance before the God who is "greater than our hearts" (3:20), whose love for us as revealed through Christ is so great that nothing can separate us from it (cf. Rom 8:38–39).

CHALLENGES OF MAINTAINING *KOINŌNIA*

One of the ironies in the New Testament is that the writings that so beautifully express fellowship and unity also reveal the painful realities of polarization, strife, and even schism. In John's Gospel, it is the evangelist's community that suffered the trauma of expulsion (as implied by the term *aposynagōgos*, "put out of the synagogue," in 9:22; 12:42; and 16:2). In the letters we are treating, the polarization, strife, and schism are internal. We saw earlier that the Elder refers to a group that "went out from us" and no longer "belong to us" (1 John 2:19). Their departure was a consequence of theological differences, here in the area of Christology. The Elder's assessment is that those who departed denied that Jesus is the Messiah (2:22). This was tantamount to failure to accept that Jesus in his humanity, and especially in his death, revealed God's love.

When we look at 2 and 3 John, we see that the struggle also played out at the level of leadership. To be sure, different assessments of Jesus and his importance remained at play (cf. 2 John 7). But what comes through more strongly is a power struggle. Third John is, in effect, a letter of recommendation for a certain Demetrius. In writing to Gaius, a leader of a house church, the Elder vouches for Demetrius's character and asks (at least implicitly) Gaius to provide for his needs (v. 12). Earlier, the Elder praises Gaius for his generous hospitality to and provisions for missionaries (likely associated with the Elder) who proclaim the gospel (vv. 5–8). Recall my earlier comment about why such hospitality in the early Christian movement was essential. So far, so good.

But then the Elder complains about a man named Diotrephes, whom he describes as one "who likes to put himself first" and "does not acknowledge our authority" (v. 9). Diotrephes, who probably was a leader in the Johannine network of communities, refuses hospitality to the Elder's emissaries. Moreover, he prevents others from extending hospitality to them (v. 10). That he has authority to do so suggests he still exercises leadership, at least over some members. The Elder is pained and upset by these developments, as the refusal of hospitality hindered the work of the gospel. It was also a personal affront.

Looking at 2 John, we see the other side of the coin. There, in a letter to the church that meets in Gaius's home, the Elder exhorts the members *not* to extend hospitality to a group of missionaries: "Do not receive into the house or welcome anyone who comes to you and does not bring this teaching [i.e., the gospel as proclaimed by the Elder]" (v. 10). To be sure, the Elder's concern is with an aberrant gospel message. But it is important to observe that the community's breakdown and mutual exclusion were the result of both theological differences and rival claims to leadership.

What do we make of all this? Doesn't this sound eerily similar in today's context? While debates about Christology are rare, there are different interpretations of and positions about doctrinal points that lead to division. There is also a divide among leaders in various churches (including the Catholic Church). We might get discouraged, thinking that some things never change. But discouragement, as St. Ignatius of Loyola taught, is not a place where God wants us to remain. Fortunately, the writings we are considering provide some helpful points of reflection.

One is by way of a negative example. We have seen that the Elder calls "antichrists" those who "went out from us" (1 John 2:18–23; 2 John 7). It is safe to assume that those people would not have regarded themselves thusly.[6] Indeed, they may very well have referred to the Elder in the same way. To say the least, this is highly charged language. Now, such language is not surprising, given that religious convictions and practices were at stake, especially when they were being challenged and opposed. But in today's religious context—whether it be intra-Church, the relationship between Christian churches, or that between religions—the use of demonizing language of others easily leads to dire consequences. One thing we can learn from the Johannine writings is to turn down the heat and refuse to employ derogatory epithets.

More positively, 2 John offers a way forward to bridge differences. A key theme in the letter is "truth" (*alētheia*), a term that occurs five times in the first four verses. As is the case with John 14:6, "truth" here refers to the revelation of God's love through Jesus, especially in his cross (and resurrection). Moreover, for the Elder, "truth" points to a way of life: "walking in the truth" (2 John 4). That is, it means conducting oneself according to the commandment of love as taught and embodied by Jesus (v. 6). The Elder thus proposes (at least implicitly) that the most eloquent witness to and proclamation of the gospel is *imitatio Christi*. Christ-like comportment can, and should, function as common ground in and between communities of faith. Although theological differences should be recognized and acknowledged, *koinōnia* can be fostered through shared *praxis* on behalf of the gospel, whether that be attending to the neediest or working for justice.

The Elder also calls for discernment of spirits (1 John 4:1–4). In the Society of Jesus, to which I belong, discernment is one of the core practices of our spirituality. More recently, the Society is calling Jesuit communities to engage in *communal* discernment. The Elder would approve. Such discernment is not easy, but it is a means of bringing people together with a common task: to listen to the Spirit and to each other as we share the fruits of our prayer. This way of coming together inculcates *koinōnia*. Communal discernment calls for humility, since the Spirit always moves ahead of us, calling us to heed and follow. Communities of faith can know they are on the right track when the criteria for their decisions are grounded in God's love as revealed through Jesus, and when those decisions promote *koinōnia* within the family of faith, especially in the midst of puzzles, paradoxes, and potentially divisive situations and issues.

QUESTIONS FOR PRAYER AND REFLECTION

1. What gospel passages or scenes most help me to appreciate how Jesus is the revelation of God's love? Of the face of God's mercy (as Pope Francis says about Jesus)?

2. How can I allow the hanging and/or wearing of a crucifix to deepen my appreciation of and gratitude for the extent of God's self-giving love revealed through Jesus?

3. How often do I reflect on the gift and dignity of being a child of God? What does this identity inspire in me? How does it affect the way I look at and treat others?

4. Whom do I find it hard to love? How can the Johannine writings help and inspire me to love better the brother and sister whom I do see? Those whom I don't see?

5. How have I experienced *koinōnia* in my community of faith? How have I contributed to that fellowship? And how am I attending to my fellowship with God and his Son?

6. What do I make of the Elder's teaching concerning sin? How can I let the beautiful image of seeing, in the life to come, God the Father as he is (1 John 3:2) motivate me to avoid sinful patterns in my life?

7. How does the Elder's statement that "perfect love casts out fear" (1 John 4:18) strike me? What are my deepest fears? How can I entrust them to Jesus?

8. What challenges do I find in praying that God's will be done in my life? How can I find and make time and space to listen more in my prayer?

9. What do I make of the divisions in the early Church? What are the obstacles to *koinōnia* in my community of faith? In my family? Among my associates?

10. To what activities that express gospel values and commitment am I attracted? How might I do them alongside others, including those whose faith community or religion is different from mine?

CHAPTER FIVE

Revelation

A
S NOTED IN THE INTRODUCTION, the Book of Revelation takes its name from the translation of the very first word of the text, *apokalypsis*. This Greek word means an "unveiling" or "disclosure" of information and truth; hence, "revelation." In this case, the disclosure is via a vision given to a man named John, who was exiled on the island of Patmos, located in the Aegean Sea.[1] John was in exile because of his witness to the gospel (Rev 1:9). His visionary experience took place "on the Lord's day" (1:10)—that is, a Sunday.

This is no ordinary revelation or disclosure, to be sure. It is "the revelation of Jesus Christ" (1:1), a phrase that signifies that it both comes *from* Jesus and is *about* Jesus. Ultimately, this revelation is *from God*. The source of the revelatory vision is the risen Lord Jesus, who appeared to John (more below) and instructed him to write down all that he was to see and then to send his text to seven churches located in Asia Minor (present-day western Turkey), including the church in Ephesus. That John was in exile for proclaiming the gospel suggests a context of persecution. That datum is supported by several details in the text, which evoke the threat, even the reality, of persecution of the churches he was instructed to address. Indeed, we will see below that this context is crucially important for understanding Revelation and for reflecting on its potential appropriation for the life of discipleship today.

In what follows, I first treat the historical context that lies behind the Book of Revelation as well as the literary genre of apocalypse. Next, I set forth what this text says about Jesus who, as risen Lord, is now "alive forever and ever" (1:18) and serves as the guarantor of God's victory over the powers of evil, sin, and death. Then I discuss the presence of prayer in this text, how it continues to be a source of the Church's prayer, and the importance of worship. Finally, I take up the description of the heavenly Jerusalem in 21:9—22:5.

HISTORICAL CONTEXT OF REVELATION AND APOCALYPSE AS A LITERARY GENRE

The Book of Revelation has evoked two very different general assessments. For some, it is the most important writing in the New Testament because it speaks about what will happen in the future. Unfortunately, the history of interpretation of Revelation reveals a tendency to *over*read one's own context and concerns into it. This tendency goes back as far as the Montanists of the second century CE.[2] A more recent example is the Branch Davidians in Waco, Texas, whose leader declared that he had decoded the seven seals of the scroll described in chapters 5—7.[3] Over the centuries, the text has inspired much violence. Moreover, there has been a temptation to identify characters in the text (e.g., the dragon and two beasts) with modern historical figures (e.g., Adolf Hitler or Saddam Hussein), which then leads to the attempt to decode other characters and symbols in the text in order to predict a particular date in the near future for the end of the world as we know it.

An essential antidote to such readings is to appreciate the *actual* historical context in which John of Patmos wrote his text. One clue involves answering the question, who is Lord and God? John insists that God, the Creator of all, is the one who is "Lord and God" (4:11) and that Jesus is "the Lord of lords and King of kings" (17:14). Why this insistence on what might seem to be an obvious claim? The Roman emperor Domitian, who ruled from 81 to 96 CE, was called by the titles *Dominus et Deus* ("Lord and God").[4] Moreover, under his rule, the imperial cult gained impetus, as did the worship of the goddess *Roma*—especially in cities eager to show Rome their loyalty. As we will see, it is most likely that John wrote in a context in which Christ-believers were being pressured to show fealty to Rome by participating in the imperial cult.

That we are on the right track is seen in how this information helps make sense of the content of 12:1—13:18, where a number of mysterious figures and symbols appear. The first "great portent" is "a woman clothed with the sun, with the moon under her feet, and on her head a crown of twelve stars" (12:1). At one level, this woman depicts Mary, who gave birth to a son "who is to rule all the nations" (12:5). At another level, she represents the Church. The second portent is "a great red dragon, with seven heads and ten horns, and seven diadems on his heads" (12:3), who attempts unsuccessfully to devour the woman's child. The dragon, whom John identifies as "the Devil and Satan, the deceiver of the whole world" (12:9), then pursues the woman, who is protected by God (12:6)—signaling both the persecution of the Church and God's protective care over it. The notice of 1,260 days functions to show that the persecution will be temporary, as God is ultimately in charge. Indeed, the dragon and his minions wage war against Michael and his angels in heaven and are defeated (12:7–9; more on this heavenly battle later).

John next describes "a beast rising out of the sea, having ten horns and seven heads; and on its horns were ten diadems, and on its heads were blasphemous names" (13:1). There follows a reference to worshiping the beast (13:4), its "uttering haughty and blasphemous words" (13:5), and its making war on "the holy ones" (au. trans. of 13:7). As is the case in Daniel 7, the beast represents a great nation and empire—here, the Roman Empire. More specifically, it stands for the Roman emperor who allowed himself to be called "Lord and God." A second beast is introduced (13:11). This one "exercises all the authority of the first beast on its behalf, and it makes the earth and its inhabitants worship the first beast" (13:12). This second beast stands for a local Roman official, likely a series of officials (e.g., in Ephesus and the other cities to whom John writes), who promoted and enforced the cult of the emperor. Putting all of this together, John wrote the Book of Revelation to churches located in cities where Christians were being pressured to abdicate their faith in the gospel in order to render worship and fealty to Roman power. The text was likely written near the end of Domitian's reign in the mid-90s CE.

It is from this context that we must first understand John's "call for the endurance and faith of the holy ones" (au. trans. of 13:10). He exhorts his readers *not* to participate in such idolatry and to persevere in the face of opposition. What follows chapters 12—13 was intended to give the seven churches confidence to trust in God's deliverance from persecution as well as to provide hope in God's faithfulness to reward the faithful righteous, especially those who were suffering—even being put to death—for their allegiance to God. Thus, the "future" depicted in Revelation was not meant to be a specific description of events to be decoded and untangled by readers centuries later. Proper interpretation and appropriation of the text must take into account this historical context.

A second assessment of Revelation, one held by many Christians today, is that it is a text that is best avoided. There is too much mysterious symbolism in it. It can be intimidating to read and difficult to understand. The history of interpretation mentioned above is discouraging. How is Revelation a life-giving text? Here is where an appreciation of the text's genre as an apocalypse can be very helpful.

Apocalyptic literature flourished in Judaism in the second and first centuries BCE and in the first century CE. The Book of Daniel in the Old Testament is an example of this literature. Features of apocalyptic literature include visions, including visions of the heavenly world, and an angelic messenger to explain them; striking and frightening images; symbolic numbers; and a view of future events. What is vitally important to appreciate is that this literature frequently emerged from contexts of suffering and persecution (e.g., the Book of Daniel was written in the early second century BCE when Antiochus IV Epiphanes was pressuring Jews to take on Greek ways, including the worship of Apollos). We might think of this literature as "insider literature." Its purpose was to offer an interpretation of history that insists that, contrary to appearances in the present, God is in charge of things and will intervene shortly to save his people and execute justice on oppressors. As such, this literature was dangerous vis-à-vis the oppressive ruling authorities. Hence the need for "insider" or coded language.

It is beyond my scope to offer here an exhaustive analysis of all the apocalyptic features of the Book of Revelation. My hope is that an appreciation of the genre, its features, and its purpose will assist readers in the sections that follow. In light of the historical context outlined above, I can offer a brief explanation of the mysterious number 666, the number of the first beast (13:18). As is the case with Latin (think Roman numerals, e.g., V = 5; X = 10), Hebrew letters have numerical values. The name *Neron Caesar*, spelled out in Hebrew letters, adds up to 666. The number points to the figure of the Roman emperor, of whom Nero—who persecuted Christians in Rome in the mid-60s—was the prototype of oppressive rule. Those marked with this number gave themselves over to the pretensions of

Domitian. As we will see, John later speaks of another mark, one given to those who have remained faithful to God.

A final word about what Revelation is and why we should value it. At the outset, John refers to his work as "the words of the prophecy" (1:3). While prophecy can refer to predictions of the future, the primary biblical sense of prophecy is that it communicates *God's* word. The Old Testament prophets often write, "Thus says the LORD...." More specifically, the message of Revelation concerns God's message as revealed by Jesus: "for the testimony of Jesus is the spirit of prophecy" (19:10). As God's word, it is living and true and thus still speaks to us today. It is to John's portrayal of the risen Jesus that we now turn.

JESUS: "THE LIVING ONE" AND "MORNING STAR"; THE SLAIN-YET-VICTORIOUS LAMB

John's first vision began with an auditory experience, as he heard a "voice like a trumpet" (1:10). Turning around, he saw "one like the Son of Man" (1:13). This figure wore a long robe with a gold sash across his chest; his hair was white as wool; his eyes burned like fire; his feet were like fire-purified bronze; his voice sounded like the roar of mighty waters; out of his mouth came a two-edged sword (signaling the word of God; cf. Heb 4:12); and his face was "like the sun shining with full force" (1:16). An imposing, even terrifying, figure! John's description draws on imagery from the Old Testament, such as Daniel 7, where the enthroned Ancient of Days (i.e., God) is described in similar ways. The effect of this vision is to reveal the heavenly and majestic glory of the risen Jesus.

The risen Jesus first identifies himself as "the first and the last, and the living one" (1:17–18). This way of self-identifying evokes how God is described in Scripture. Indeed, we will see how the risen Jesus shares the very throne of God. He goes on to reveal something crucially important: "I was dead, and see, I am alive forever and ever" (1:18). Jesus's resurrection (and ascension into glory) is the decisive moment of God's victory over Satan and over the powers of evil, sin, and death. It is this victory that assures the recipients of Revelation that they will share in it if they persevere and remain faithful to God and God's ways. Suffering and death do not have the last word.

Revelation is unique among apocalypses in that it is told from the side of God's victory *already* accomplished. Recall the mention earlier of the heavenly battle between Michael and his angels versus Satan (symbolized by the dragon) and his minions (12:7–9). Another feature of apocalypses is that what happens in heaven will eventually play out in space and time in the world. This brief reference to the heavenly battle is another way of communicating that, though sin and evil are still among us, they will not overcome—an important message to those who are suffering persecution and are discouraged. The risen Jesus, "the bright morning star" (22:16), shines through the darkness of tribulations, showing forth the promise of everlasting life.

While John highlights the glorious majesty of the risen Lord, he does not lose sight of Jesus's saving death on the cross. John received a vision of "a Lamb standing as if it had been slaughtered, having seven horns and seven eyes" (5:6). In the background here is the suffering servant of Isaiah 53 (cf. "like a lamb that is led to the slaughter"; Isa 53:7). The glorified one is also the crucified one, through whose blood God has ransomed people from every language and nation (Rev 5:9). That the Lamb has seven horns and seven eyes is symbolism to indicate that the risen Lord is all-powerful (the horns) and all-knowing (the eyes). Sharing the throne of God, the Lamb now acts as *shepherd* (John can mix his metaphors!), guiding those who were faithful to the end to "springs of the water of life" (7:17). As we will see in the final section, the Lamb along with the "Lord God the Almighty" will be in the midst of the heavenly Jerusalem, giving light to all (21:22–23).

The image of Jesus as the slain-yet-victorious Lamb can help us understand better what John means by the aforementioned phrase "for the testimony of Jesus is the spirit of prophecy" (19:10). The word rendered "testimony" is *martyria*. One can easily see the word *martyr* contained therein. In fact, *martyr* comes from the Greek *martys*, whose primary meaning is "witness" or "testifier." Jesus, the "Faithful and True" (19:11), bore witness to the saving love of God by giving his life on the cross. John's exhortation to his readers to endure in fidelity to God in the face of pressure from opposing forces is a call to bear witness to the gospel. For some, it meant bearing witness with their own blood. Such dramatic witness is not just a thing of the past. St. Oscar Romero is a contemporary example of such witness—called martyrdom.

This portrayal of Jesus is important to keep in mind when we come to another image toward the end of the book, that of the rider on the white horse who leads out the armies of heaven into victorious battle (19:11–16). This divine warrior is described as having eyes "like a flame of fire" (19:12). His robe has been dipped in blood (19:13) and "from his mouth comes a sharp sword with which to strike down the nations," over whom he will rule "with a rod of iron" (19:15). He will do so as "King of kings and Lord of lords" (19:16). Now, this hardly sounds like "the Prince of Peace" (cf. Isa 9:6), the one portrayed in the Gospels as "gentle and humble in heart" (Matt 11:29; cf. 21:5) and who taught nonviolent resistance and love of enemies (Matt 5:38–48), does it?

It appears that John drew much of this imagery from Isaiah 63:1–3[5] but with some significant variations. Jesus the divine warrior goes to battle with blood *already* on his garment. This is not the blood of his enemies (as in Isaiah) but his own blood, the blood poured forth in his sacrificial death that has brought ransom and salvation (Rev 5:9). His name is "The Word of God" (19:13) because he has revealed, as the slain-yet-victorious Lamb, God's power through self-giving love. The "sword" he wields is the proclamation of the gospel, which is the offer of life to those who accept it, the only true "life" there is (which makes its rejection so tragic). I want to be careful not to water down John's image of the divine warrior, but it's important to appreciate that he uses it to *encourage* his readers who were faced with persecution from governing authorities. John assures them that the power of love revealed by the true Lord and King overcomes the powers of evil, sin, and death. And as we will see in the final section, his "rule" will be marked by peace and security from those powers.

One final image of Jesus that John offers is one with which you are likely familiar. It is the description of the risen Lord who, in his own words, declares, "Listen! I am standing at the door, knocking; if you hear my voice and open the door, I will come in to you and eat with you, and you with me" (3:20). What a beautiful image! The risen Lord knocking at the door of our hearts. As the revelation of God's love, Jesus *invites* his way in; he doesn't force himself on us. He is the one who takes the initiative to draw us into greater intimacy with him. That is how grace works. Having an intimate dinner with a loved one or friend is a special experience. No wonder the risen Lord appeals to that experience here. He truly wants to be our *companion* (the word derives from sharing bread with another).

Of course, one way in which we can welcome Jesus into our hearts is through frequent reception of the Eucharist. Also, through prayerful reflection on God's word (which I hope this book is facilitating). In order to hear Jesus knocking at the door of our hearts, we need to listen, to take time for quiet in prayer. The Book of Revelation is a great source of prayer, both for our private prayer and especially in the Church's communal (i.e., liturgical) prayer. Indeed, this text suggests much about the importance of prayer and worship in the life of discipleship.

THE IMPORTANCE OF PRAYER AND WORSHIP IN THE BOOK OF REVELATION

Selected readings from the Book of Revelation are proclaimed at two particular times of the year in the Church's eucharistic liturgy: in the second reading on the Sundays of Easter in Year C; and in the first reading at the weekday Masses during the last two weeks of Ordinary Time in Year II.[6] That lections from this text are proclaimed in the Easter season is most appropriate, because it proclaims the words of the *risen* Lord. That Revelation is read during the final weeks of Ordinary Time is very fitting, since those celebrations point us to the "last things," reminding us that God is leading history to its climactic conclusion.

In addition to having a place in the Church's liturgical proclamation of God's word, Revelation is a rich source for the Church's prayer—especially in the Liturgy of the Hours, often referred to as the Breviary. The Breviary is the set of prayers that mark the hours of the day (e.g., early morning, midday, evening, nighttime). If you have ever been to a monastery, these are the prayers the monks or nuns pray, often accompanied by music. The Psaltery of the Breviary contains, in addition to the Psalms, "canticles" from the Old and New Testaments. The New Testament canticles are prayed in Evening Prayer (known as "Vespers"). Four of the seven New Testament canticles, one of which is prayed every evening during the week, are taken from Revelation.[7] In what follows, I offer a glance at these four canticles, which will function as a way to review and point to some major themes of the text.

Before doing so, it is important to recognize that these

canticles are revealed in the context of John's being transported into heaven (Rev 4:1). Visions of heaven are a feature of apocalyptic literature. John was shown the throne on which God is seated in glorious majesty, surrounded by twenty-four enthroned elders and "four living creatures" who worship God "day and night without ceasing" (4:2–11). Other heavenly visions show countless faithful people (the holy ones) singing praises before God (e.g., 15:2–3). In other words, what was revealed to John is the heavenly liturgy, the eternal liturgy in which we can participate now in the present.

Let's start with the canticle in the Breviary prayed on Tuesdays (Rev 4:11; 5:9–10, 12), which is actually a compilation of three short songs. It is a prayer directed both to God (4:11) and to the risen Jesus, who has just been revealed as the slain-yet-victorious Lamb (5:9). It is no accident that the hymn begins with the address, "Our Lord and God." Recall that the emperor Domitian was wont to receive these acclamations. The hymn insists, however, that these titles belong only to the Creator God and the risen Lord Jesus. It goes on to sing of the shedding of the Lamb's blood, through which he "ransomed for God holy ones from every...people and nation" (au. trans. of 5:9). Jesus's saving death has universal effects. Moreover, the people so redeemed have been made "to be a kingdom and priests serving our God" (5:10).[8] As we saw in 1 Peter, *all* the baptized members of the Church have a priestly identity. One responsibility and privilege of priests (lay and ordained) is to pray. With his canticles, John has provided the Church with some beautiful prayers.

The second canticle—joining together parts of two songs (11:17–18; 12:10b–12a) and prayed on Thursdays—is a hymn that praises God for his defeat of sin and evil and sings of the victory of salvation of those martyrs whose faithfulness to the gospel cost them their lives. The first part of the canticle presages the final judgment ("the time for judging the dead") that will include "rewarding" those, "both small and great," who remain faithful to the end (11:18). The second part sings of the coming of salvation and the full manifestation of "the kingdom of our God and the authority of his Messiah," following upon the defeat of Satan ("for the accuser of our brothers and sisters has been thrown down"; au. trans. of 12:10; cf. 12:7–9). Fear of death did not deter those who have conquered through "the blood of the Lamb and by the word of their testimony" (12:11). This canticle bears witness to God's vindication of martyrs—a message that strengthened John's readers, and one that still communicates a word of hope today.

The third canticle, prayed on Fridays, is a brief hymn of praise (15:3–4). "Lord God the Almighty" is honored for his "great and amazing" deeds and for his ways that are "just and true." God alone is holy, the one and only one to whom the nations will come in worship. This hymn is called "the song of Moses," because it celebrates—à la the original exodus (Exod 15:1–18)—the liberation (i.e., redemption) from slavery to sin and death that God has brought through the death and resurrection of Jesus. Therefore, it is also called "the song of the Lamb."

This simple yet profound canticle invites reflection on the topic of worship. On two occasions in the text, John is so overcome with the visions and awed by the angel who explains them that he falls down to worship the heavenly being (Rev 19:10; 22:8–9). He is immediately told to worship God and God alone. The implications of this for his readers were clear: they were not to participate in the cult of the emperor or the worship of the goddess *Roma*. But what about us today? How might we reflect on the relevance of the command to worship God and God alone?

Like the original readers of Revelation, our prayer to God—personal and especially communal—connects us with the heavenly realities. We are strengthened to participate here and now in the fruits of the salvation won for us by the slain-yet-victorious Lamb. Although we may not experience opposition and persecution like John's audience did, we do need help for the journey. Taking the time to worship God is a healthy and honest acknowledgment of this need and of our trust in God to lead and support us to persevere in the life of faith by bearing testimony (*martyria*) with our lives to the gospel.

In addition, worship of God—and God alone—is salutary for resisting the various ways in which our total allegiance can be demanded by sources that are not God. Although the Roman Empire has been long gone, the dynamics of powerful nationalistic and political forces and ideologies continue today. These can demand a loyalty and adherence to things that are in tension with, even in opposition to, the ways of God as revealed through Christ. Regular participation in the Church's liturgy is a healthy remedy against the totalizing demands of such forces and ideologies, as we declare our wholehearted fealty to God and let him form our fundamental convictions and priorities.

Worship of the one who alone is holy (Rev 15:4) can also prevent us from falling into various forms of idolatry. It is easy to allow things like the acquisition and protection of material possessions, the attainment of professional status, or the pursuit of interests and hobbies to take up inordinate amounts of our time, passion, and energy. They can unwittingly become "idols." The same can be true of some human relationships. What or whom do I find myself focusing on, dreaming about, and pursuing in my discretionary time and with my discretionary resources? The answer(s) to this question can be revealing. To be sure, these can be good things. But if they lead me away from acknowledging God as the source of true life and happiness, and away from taking time to pray to and worship God, I could be succumbing to a form of idolatry. Worship of God is a good corrective to such tendencies.

The fourth New Testament canticle from Revelation in the Breviary, sung by "a great multitude in heaven," glorifies God as the true King and announces "the marriage of the Lamb" to a bride who has been made ready for him (19:1–7). This canticle leads us to the dramatic conclusion of the Book of Revelation: the vision of the new Jerusalem.

THE HEAVENLY JERUSALEM (21:9—22:5)

To speak of a "conclusion" to Revelation raises the question about its storyline. What is the "plot" in the text to which the vision of the new Jerusalem is the conclusion? To be sure, one can experience a jarring sense of what seems to be endless repetitions: the scroll with seven seals that are then broken; seven trumpets; seven angels with the seven bowls of plagues. Indeed, there is no straight or linear storyline told in Revelation. But there *is* a movement forward. Notice that the slain-yet-victorious Lamb, the only one found "worthy" to break open the seven seals (5:9), *continues* to be an active character. This is John's way of referring to God's definitive action, one that will bring divine judgment against the forces of evil, sin, and death and that will bring the fullness of salvation to those who remain faithful. God is in charge of things, even if it might not be evident, especially for those who suffer persecution.

In the context of John's original readers, the judgment against Rome, the city set on seven hills (17:9), communicated to them the imminent defeat of the source of their opposition and persecution. Chapters 17—18 describe the judgment against the power of Rome—portrayed in a vision as a drunken harlot on a scarlet beast and referred to as Babylon (the archetypal enemy of God's people)—and its subsequent fall, as well as the lament of all who associated with her. The lament ends, "In you was found the blood of prophets and of holy ones" (au. trans. of 18:24). Then John heard a victory song sung by "a great multitude in heaven," celebrating God's judgment against "the great whore" (19:1–3) and proclaiming the full coming of God's reign and the marriage of the Lamb to a bride (19:6–8).

Reference to a bride brings us to the final vision in Revelation (21:9—22:5).[9] Given its placement in the canon, this is also the final vision in the entire Bible. An angelic figure takes John in spirit to a mountain, saying, "Come, I will show you the bride, the wife of the Lamb" (21:9; cf. 21:2). And what does John see? "The holy city Jerusalem coming down out of heaven from God" (21:10)! A bride that's a city? What's going on here? In the first place, cities were symbolized by women. We just saw how John portrayed Rome as a harlot. Now he draws on the tradition of Jerusalem as personified "daughter Zion" (Lam 1:6). That the city coming from heaven is called "Jerusalem" is significant because it represents the longing of God's people to be in his presence (see, e.g., Ps 122).

The city John saw is no ordinary city. It is a walled city whose foundations are "adorned with every jewel" (Rev 21:19). The twelve gates of the city are pearls, and the main thoroughfare is "pure gold, transparent as glass" (21:21). Through the city runs a "river of the water of life, bright as crystal, flowing from the throne of God and of the Lamb" (22:1). There is much to take in here, to say the least! This city gleams with beauty. A walled city is a place of security, where people can dwell in safety and without fear (cf. Ps 107:4–7). No one or nothing that could bring harm to the inhabitants can get in (cf. Rev 21:27).

Even more conspicuous is the *size* of the city, whose length and width are twelve thousand *stadia* (i.e., ca. fifteen hundred miles)! The area contained therein is equivalent to the size of the civilized world around the Mediterranean (the world known by John of Patmos). What this communicates is that in "the life of the world to come" (Nicene Creed), there will be multitudes of people. Much space is required for the "great multitude in heaven" (19:1), a multitude from "every tribe and language and people and nation" (5:9). Recall the expansive reach of the Lamb's redeeming blood (cf., also, 1 Tim 2:4). Eternal life is not merely a personal and private experience of God. Rather, it is *communal*, the fullness of the manifestation of the people of God. People will bring into it "the glory and honor" of their cultures, the best of all human traditions (cf. Rev 21:26).

While John's imagery highlights what we might call urban and societal aspects, it also includes elements of nature. Alongside the river of living waters grow trees that produce fresh fruit monthly and whose leaves are medicinal. What John suggests thereby is similar to what St. Paul teaches: "the creation itself will be set free from its bondage to decay and will obtain the freedom of the glory of the children of God" (Rom 8:21). That is, nature will be integrated into the life to come as an essential part of the new creation, "a new heaven and a new earth" (Rev 21:1).

The most striking feature of John's vision—indeed, what is most important—is the presence of God and of the Lamb, enthroned in the middle of the city (Rev 22:3). Unlike cities of old, this city has no temple building. Why? "Its temple is the Lord God the Almighty and the Lamb" (21:22). Here is the quintessential image of eternal life: God dwelling in person in the midst of all his people. This dwelling enacts what God foreshadowed when his Son, the Word, "became flesh and lived among us" (John 1:14). Recall that this vision began by identifying the new Jerusalem as "a bride adorned for her husband" (Rev 21:2). God's presence with all his holy people is an expression of divine intimacy for all his people and creation.

God and the risen Lord are the suppliers of all the light that is needed. In the new Jerusalem "there will be no more night" (22:5). The absence of sun and stars means there is no way to mark the passing of time and seasons. This is John's way of expressing that life with God is *eternal*. Those who have been faithful will worship before God's throne and "will see his face" (22:4; cf. 1 John 3:2). God "will wipe every tear from their eyes. / Death will be no more; / mourning and crying and pain will be no more" (Rev 21:4). Those who see God will be marked with the divine name on their foreheads (and not 666), for they belong to him and now enjoy his everlasting love and protection.

Such is the vision that concludes the Book of Revelation—and the Bible as a whole. This is the way God will bring history to its intended end. When? As we saw in 2 Peter, God acts in his time, not by our timelines. This is why it is crucially important to understand what the Book of Revelation is and what it intends to communicate: not a set of mysterious clues portending the end of history as we know it, clues we are to unravel, but rather the promise of God to defeat definitively the forces of evil, sin, and death. Even more, John reveals his inspiring visionary experience of eternal life in the presence of the living God and of the slain-yet-victorious Lamb, where the faithful sing God's praises in loving worship in the New Jerusalem. What an ending!

QUESTIONS FOR PRAYER AND REFLECTION

1. How does the historical context of Revelation and its literary genre as an apocalypse help me to understand this text better?

2. For those of us who are not living in a context of persecution, how can this writing speak to me in my present circumstances?

3. How can I allow the revelation of the risen Lord as the one who, though once dead, is now "alive forever and ever" (1:18) to increase my hope and trust in God's resurrection power?

4. What can I do to hear and respond to the risen Jesus who stands knocking at the door of my heart? How is he drawing me into greater intimacy with him?

5. How might the appreciation that our communal liturgical prayer (e.g., Mass and the Breviary) is a participation in the heavenly liturgy revealed in Revelation change my experience of communal prayer?

6. How does John's emphasis on the importance of proper worship inspire me? Challenge me?

7. Which of the New Testament canticles taken from Revelation do I prefer? Why?

8. Why is it significant that the entire Bible ends with John's vision of the new Jerusalem? What have I learned from that vision? What surprises me?

9. Given what John reveals about the diversity of peoples who will inhabit the heavenly city, how am I challenged today to regard others who are different from me?

10. Given the redemption of creation and nature as set forth by John's vision and by Romans 8, how might I be inspired to embrace more enthusiastically Pope Francis's teachings about the care for creation in *Laudato Si'*?

Conclusion

H AVING TRAVERSED AND EXPLORED Hebrews, the Catholic Epistles, and Revelation, it will be helpful to take stock of some of the highlights we have encountered. I cannot offer here a thorough review; however, a brief summary of themes, topics, and images we would miss were it not for the content of these less traveled texts can be beneficial.

These writings contain some important theological teachings. That is, they reveal to us significant information about who God is and what God wants for us. James's description of God as "the Father of lights, with whom there is no variation or shadow due to change" (Jas 1:17), aptly communicates divine transcendence. His teaching that God "gives to all generously and ungrudgingly" (1:5) speaks to the expansive quality of divine munificence. James also reminds us of God's special love and concern for the poor (2:5). The Johannine epistles teach us just how generous God is: "God sent his only Son into the world so that we might live through him" (1 John 4:9). And all this because, as the Elder so famously expressed, "God is love" (4:8, 16), a theological statement unsurpassed for its succinctness and profundity.

The less traveled texts have also revealed God's desire to be in relationship with us. Readers will have noticed how frequently I have used the word *covenantal* to describe God. As

Eucharistic Prayer III so beautifully puts it, "you [God] never cease to gather a people to yourself." Even more, God desires to draw close to us. The Elder emphasizes that God did so in the incarnation of his Son and through the bestowal of the gift of the Spirit, through whom God abides in us and we in him (1 John 3:24). Moreover, in his introduction to his final vision, that of the new Jerusalem, John of Patmos beautifully sets forth in a hymn this divine impetus to be with God's people: "See, the home of God is among mortals. / He will dwell with them; / they will be his peoples, / and God himself will be with them" (Rev 21:3). The transcendent God is no detached "divine clockmaker" who long ago set things in motion and now watches from a distance. God is involved in his creation and history. And eternal life means living and worshiping—in community with all God's faithful—in the very presence of God.

Moreover, these texts highlight God's salvific action through the death and resurrection of Jesus. This salvific action entails forgiveness and cleansing from sin, as well as redemption. A review of the preceding chapters shows many such notices. For our purposes here, let's focus on what these writings teach about Jesus and his saving death. The author of Hebrews details Jesus's priestly identity via "the order of Melchizedek" (Heb 6:20). In this text, Jesus is both priest and sacrifice. As high priest, it is his own blood that he brought, once for all, into the heavenly Holy Place, the blood that has effected "eternal redemption" (9:12). Similarly, Peter writes of the ransoming "blood of Christ, like that of a lamb without defect or blemish" (1 Pet 1:19). And John of Patmos recounts his vision of the slain-yet-victorious Lamb (Rev 5:6).

Indeed, the less traveled texts greatly enrich the Christology of the New Testament. While Paul refers to Jesus as the one "who is at the right hand of God, who...intercedes for us" (Rom 8:34), it is the author of Hebrews who fills out this image of the glorious Christ as our intercessor before the Father. The risen

Lord thereby *continues* to exercise his ministry as high priest. Having "become like his brothers and sisters in every respect" (Heb 2:17), and having been "tested as we are," he is now a merciful and compassionate high priest, one before whom we can approach "with boldness, so that we may receive mercy and find grace to help in time of need" (4:15–16). Jesus was like we are in every respect—except for sin, that is. The texts less traveled insist on the sinlessness of Jesus (Heb 4:15; 7:26; 1 Pet 1:19; 2:22; 3:18; and 1 John 3:5). It was as "pioneer and perfecter of our faith" (Heb 12:2) that he has taken his seat at God's right hand, because he endured the cross for the sake of the glory and joy that awaited him.

Revelation provides the risen Jesus's own testimony that death has no more power over him (Rev 1:18). His resurrection and ascension are the assurance and proof of God's victory over the powers of evil, sin, and death. It is this writing that also brings to us the beautiful image of the Lord's knocking at the door of our hearts, waiting to be let in so that he may commune with us (3:20). Truly, the less traveled texts enhance and deepen our appreciation of Jesus's ongoing ways of ministering to us—that is, of his continuing to be *for* us.

These texts also supply important images of the Church. The author of Hebrews (cf., e.g., Heb 11:8–10), with his emphasis on God's people as sojourners, provides the basis for Vatican II's presentation of the Church as a pilgrim people. Indeed, I hope that this book has provided sustenance for the journey that we make as individuals and as a community. Peter takes up an image found in Ephesians 2:19–22 and refers to Christians as "living stones" built on the cornerstone that is Christ (1 Pet 2:4–8), a "building" that is the dwelling place of the Holy Spirit. These "living stones," by virtue of their baptism, are a priestly people (2:9) who offer spiritual sacrifices. John of Patmos confirms this priestly identity of *all* God's people (Rev

5:10). One way to enact this priesthood is by praying, and John has provided the Church with canticles of praise.

The covenantal God not only calls a people to be in relationship with him. God also *forms* a people, who are to grow in and show forth God's holiness to others (e.g., 1 Pet 1:15–16, which quotes Lev 19:2, "You shall be holy, for I [the LORD your God] am holy"). While each of the writings offers instruction on what holiness looks like, James provides the "big picture" in his description of "the wisdom from above" (Jas 3:17–18) and his teaching on the "royal law" (2:8), the way of life taught and enacted by Jesus. James also insists that the life of faith must be animated by works, especially what we today call the works of mercy (2:14–26). He teaches that friendship with God entails sharing the divine love and care for the poor. "Pure" religion is "to care for orphans and widows in their distress, and to keep oneself unstained by the world" (1:27).

The Elder employs the imagery of family to describe the Church, whose members are God's sons and daughters (1 John 3:1). As members of God's family in whom "God's seed" (i.e., the gift of the Spirit) abides (3:9), we are to grow and mature in taking on the divine "family likeness"—namely, self-giving love. Moreover, as members of God's family, we are to live and embody the *koinōnia* ("fellowship") that God's love creates, thereby bearing witness to the world that God sent his only Son to reveal the divine love (cf. John 17:21).

The Elder's reference to the family of God includes a future orientation: "we are God's children now; what we will be has not yet been revealed. What we do know is this: when he is revealed, we will be like him, for we will see him as he is" (1 John 3:2). Here is an allusion to "the life of the world to come" (the final words of the Nicene Creed). A theme that pervades the less traveled texts is *hope*, which is tantamount to being a leitmotif of this book. The definition of *faith* given by the author of Hebrews pertains to all of these writings: "faith is the assurance of things hoped for, the conviction of things not seen" (Heb 11:1).

Christian hope is grounded, as we have seen repeatedly, in the resurrection and ascension of Jesus. So too it is rooted in the conviction that God has been, and continues to be, involved in his creation and in history. Peter and John of Patmos insist on this point. Peter's strong response to the "scoffers" rested in the firm belief in the resurrection of the dead and in the confidence that history is moving toward a divinely appointed and guided conclusion (cf. 2 Pet 3:1–10).

It is surely no accident that the Book of Revelation, and the New Testament as a whole, ends with John's divinely given vision of the new Jerusalem (Rev 21:9—22:5). This beautiful vision of God's personal presence in the midst of his faithful people—within the beauty and security of an immensely large jewel-walled, gold-paved city—is the *telos*, the culmination and goal, of God's work of creation and redemption. It provides us a good start for preparing to give a response to those who ask for the basis of our hope (1 Pet 3:15).

As I have worked my way through the less traveled texts in writing this book—doing so in the context of a worldwide pandemic, outcries for racial justice, and seemingly endless social polarizations—I have been struck by the need today to bear witness to hope. Not a "pie in the sky" hope, but hope that lives out of deep resurrection faith and trust in God to fulfill the divine promises. Such hope inspires one to offer oneself, each and every day, as a disciple of Jesus, to be a son or daughter of God whose love becomes more expansive, who is committed more and more to justice in its various forms—social, political, racial, economic, and environmental—so that God's kingdom may be realized more and more on earth as it is in heaven. Such hope enables one to offer one's sufferings in union with the sufferings of Christ, through whose suffering and death God has brought salvation. That is, such hope facilitates the ongoing outworking of the paschal mystery.

This book began by referring to Frost's poem "The Road Not Taken." In the final stanza the poet places himself in the future "somewhere ages and ages hence," from which he looks back on a walk in the woods. We have taken a journey through texts that, in their climax, point us to a glorious future. And it is our hope in God's promises and life-giving power, lived out in the manner suggested above, that *can* make "all the difference"—in our own lives, in our Church, and in our world.

Notes

PREFACE

1. The entire poem, with an audio reading, can be accessed at https://www.poetryfoundation.org/poems/44272/the-road-not-taken (accessed December 1, 2021).

2. These texts are also called "Catholic" because they were eventually recognized as inspired writings by the larger (i.e., Catholic) Church, and thus as part of the New Testament canon.

3. Seven letters—Romans, 1 and 2 Corinthians, Galatians, Philippians, 1 Thessalonians, and Philemon—are considered by scholars as undisputedly from Paul. Three others—Ephesians, Colossians, and 2 Thessalonians—are "disputed," meaning that some scholars claim they were written after the Apostle's death, in the spirit and tradition of Paul's teaching, to address new situations. The other three, the so-called Pastoral Epistles—1 and 2 Timothy, Titus—are regarded by most scholars to be penned well after the time of Paul.

4. See, e.g., David Orr, *The Road Not Taken: Finding America in the Poem Everyone Loves and Almost Everyone Gets Wrong* (New York: Penguin, 2015).

CHAPTER ONE—HEBREWS

1. Scholars observe in this text significant differences in vocabulary, writing style, and theological outlook from those found in Paul's letters. I will refer to the writer of Hebrews as "the author" and use masculine pronouns (though it is possible, as some conjecture, that the author was a woman).

2. The divine passive refers to the use of a verb in passive voice without a named subject in order to indicate that *God* is the agent who acts. It reflects Jewish reverence for God and God's holy name.

3. The NRSV's commendable commitment to use inclusive language in Heb 2:6 ("human beings" instead of "man"; "mortals" instead of "son of man") obscures the exegetical point made by the author.

4. To be sure, the author does not deny Jesus's fleshly existence or the importance of our earthly lives. The Platonism found in Hebrews is thereby mitigated in a significant way.

5. The NRSV renders *hagioi* as "saints" (e.g., 6:10). "Holy ones" is preferable, since in Catholic circles the word "saint" typically connotes one who has been formally canonized after death.

6. In chapter 3, we will take up the topic of how our suffering—including that from illness and diminishment—can be offered to God through Jesus in participation in the paschal mystery.

CHAPTER TWO—JAMES

1. He is likely the James who is listed in Mark 6:3 among Jesus's brothers. "Brother" here has a broader reference than blood brother. This James may be Jesus's cousin or stepbrother.

2. I am indebted to Prof. Johnson for much of what I know about the Epistle of James. For a detailed explanation

of his reading of James 4:5, see *The Letter of James: A New Translation with Commentary*, Anchor Bible 37A (New York: Doubleday, 1995), 267, 280–82.

3. What complicates things is that the same word, *peirasmos*, can mean enticement to sin as well as a testing of one's character. James uses the word in the second sense in 1:2, where "trials" are a source of testing one's faith.

4. A (hypothesized) written source of materials used by Matthew and Luke, called the "Q Source," was a collection of sayings of Jesus.

5. The NRSV has the translation "through the faith of Jesus Christ" in a footnote as a possible rendering. This captures better Paul's meaning than "through faith in Jesus Christ."

6. Erasmus proposed changing *phoneuete* ("you murder") to *phthoneite* ("you envy") in his critical Greek edition of the New Testament.

CHAPTER THREE—1 AND 2 PETER (JUDE)

1. The author of this letter identifies himself as "Jude… brother of James," the latter likely a reference to the figure who authored the text discussed in chapter 2 (cf. the list of Jesus's "brothers" in Mark 6:3). Most scholars consider this letter to be penned in the name of Jude, similar to how 2 Peter was written in the name of Peter. Readers should appreciate that pseudonymous writing was a common practice at the time.

2. A comparison between Jude 5–16 and 2 Pet 2:2–12 reveals that the latter "edits" Jude's list of examples of false teachers, many of which are taken from Scripture, in two significant ways. First, the events to which 2 Peter refers are put in the order in which they appear in the biblical canon; second, references to extrabiblical sources (e.g., to *1 Enoch* and to the no longer extant *Assumption of Moses*) are omitted. I will

focus, in the last section of this chapter, on Peter's confronting specific false teachings.

3. Hence, I refer to the author of both writings as "Peter."

4. The other three "servant songs" are Isa 42:1–7; 49:1–6; and 50:4–9. Fittingly, all four are proclaimed in the Church's eucharistic liturgy during Holy Week.

5. Nearly two years have passed between my typing this section heading and writing the following paragraphs. My work was interrupted by emergency surgery to remove a glioblastoma from my right frontal lobe. I have undergone two craniotomies (a second cancerous tumor recently emerged). This condition has given me ample opportunity to reflect on suffering and on how to find meaning in it. I hope this section is better than it would have been without this interruption.

6. This prayer can be accessed at http://www.ciszek .org/Additional_Prayers.html. Ciszek, a Polish American Jesuit priest, was ministering clandestinely in the Soviet Union when he was arrested as a Vatican "spy" in 1941. For years he suffered imprisonment, torture, isolation, and (later) hard labor in the Russian gulags.

7. First Thessalonians 4:17 suggests that Paul thought it would occur in his lifetime.

CHAPTER FOUR—1, 2, AND 3 JOHN

1. Hence, I'll refer to the author of all three as "the Elder."

2. If this writing, as most scholars contend, is late first century CE, the Elder was truly that, an older man. Old age, with the wisdom it accrues, was highly respected and appreciated.

3. It is significant to note that the entirety of 1 John is read at the weekday liturgies during the Christmas season, which

is not a surprise given the importance of the incarnation in its presentation.

4. This emphasis in John's Gospel and 1 John is the impetus behind the annual celebration of the Week of Prayer for Christian Unity in January.

5. In Greek (the original language of the New Testament), there is a relationship between the verbs *obey* (*hypakouō*) and *listen* (*akouō*). Intense listening to God that allows his word to permeate us more and more produces obedience to his ways.

6. Similarly, the monikers "strong" and "weak" in Romans 14—15 were likely the creation of the former.

CHAPTER FIVE—REVELATION

1. Hence, the author is often called John of Patmos. This John is probably a different figure from the author to whom the Fourth Gospel is attributed (*Iōannēs*, "John," was a common name). I will refer to the author of the Book of Revelation simply as John.

2. The Montanists were a group that claimed special access to the Spirit and prophetic powers, associated with a mountain they identified as the mount from which John of Patmos received the vision of the new Jerusalem (cf. Rev 21:10).

3. To be sure, there is much more complexity behind the tragedy of the 1993 siege of the Branch Davidian compound in Waco, Texas, a siege that left eighty-six people dead.

4. Historians debate whether or not Domitian officially decreed these titles for himself.

5. This passage describes in vivid language the divine wrath against those who oppose God.

6. The Sunday Lectionary has a three-year cycle of readings (A, B, and C); the Weekday Lectionary has a two-year cycle

(I, in years ending in an odd number; and II, in years ending in an even number).

7. The other three are Phil 2:6–11; Eph 1:3–10; Col 1:12–20, all of which are "Christ hymns." While priests and religious take a vow to pray the Breviary (the prayer of and for the Church) every day, *all* Catholics are encouraged to pray it, especially Morning Prayer and Evening Prayer. Indeed, it is a precious resource for prayer.

8. Unless otherwise noted, I retain the translation of the NRSV (which differs slightly from the translation approved for the Breviary) in this section.

9. In the treatment that follows, I am greatly indebted to the interpretation of this vision offered by Gerhard Lohfink, *Is This All There Is? On Resurrection and Eternal Life*, trans. L. M. Maloney (Collegeville, MN: Liturgical Press, 2018), 194–202.